The New York Times

On the Web

CROSSWORDS FOR TEENS

Puzzles by Frank Longo
Edited by Will Shortz

ST. MARTIN'S GRIFFIN ✾ NEW YORK

www.stmartins.com

ISBN 978-0-312-28911-9

First Edition: February 2002

Introduction

WHAT'S PUZZLING YOU?

Where would you be if you were in the capital of Latvia (Famous Artist and Works, 54-Across)? What is the energy source of the solar system (Electricity and Magnetism, 30-Down)? Who is Homer Simpson's famous wife (The Electoral Process, 46-Down)? We knew when we started out to make a crossword puzzle book for teens that it had to be fun and educational—something that a teacher would use and that students would love. We looked around for similar books on the market, but imagine our suprise when we couldn't find a single one! You hold in your hands the only crossword puzzle book that is fun, educational, and just for teens!

The crossword puzzles in these pages are some of the most popular crosswords found on the *New York Times* Learning Network, a site from *The New York Times* on the Web for teachers, students, and parents. Every two weeks, the *Times* "puzzlemasters" (the guys who create the world-famous crosswords for *The New York Times* everyday) create a new puzzle for teens based on interesting themes like Music, 20th Century Innovations, and Authors and Literature. These puzzles will challenge what you know about these topics and test your "word smarts" in all of the clues, from RIGA to the SUN to MARGE.

Thousands of kids and teachers are doing these crosswords around the world. These puzzles are one of The Learning Network's most popular features, averaging about 200,000 "page views" each month.

If you like what you see in this book, go online and play some more, either right there on your screen or printed out on paper! Just go to: http://www.nytimes.com/learning/teachers/xwords. Or if you want to explore all of the site's fantastic features for kids your age, such as the Who's Who & What's What daily news quiz, Ask a Reporter, On This Day in History, Test Prep Question of the Day, and Web Explorer, go to http://www.nytimes.com/learning.

Now, go get puzzled!

Alison Zimbalist
Education Editor
The New York Times on the Web

THE 50 STATES

ACROSS

1. _____ of 10,000 Lakes (nickname for Minnesota)
5. The Silver State
11. Newhart or Hope of comedy
14. Vase-shaped pitcher
15. Country singer Krauss
16. Numbered highway: Abbr.
17. Nickname for Virginia: 2 wds.
19. "The Addams Family" cousin
20. Regret bitterly
21. Deviate from a straight course, as a ship or plane
22. Occupied a chair
23. Strongboxes for valuables
26. Boxer's combination punch: 2 wds.
29. Rapper _____ Kim
30. State tree of Tennessee, Indiana and Kentucky: 2 wds.
35. State flower of Tennessee
37. Sandal or sneaker
38. Frozen stuff plentiful in Alaska
39. _____ support (help for computer users)
40. Person cutting down a tree, for example
42. Prefix meaning "eight"
45. Kit _____ (candy bar)
47. Put money in the bank
48. Praise highly
49. State tree of Massachusetts and North Dakota: 2 wds.
53. Org. with the Utah Jazz
54. Sheep valued for its fine wool
55. The _____ State (Rhode Island)
57. Phone number addition: Abbr.
58. Long _____ (way back when)
61. Santa _____, California
62. MTV hostess Peeples
63. Arizona tourist attraction: 2 wds.
68. Caesar's 601
69. Self-_____ (pride)
70. Prefix with dynamic or space
71. Do, re, mi, fa, _____, la, ti, do
72. Space _____ (tourist attraction in Seattle, Washington)
73. The _____ Frontier (nickname for Alaska)

DOWN

1. Actor DiCaprio, for short
2. Leather-piercing tool
3. Homer's neighbor on "The Simpsons"
4. Gangsta rapper who's Eminem's producer: 2 wds.
5. On a first-_____ basis
6. Yale student
7. Abounding in climbing plants
8. Cambodia's continent
9. 1950's music style: Hyph.
10. Advice columnist Landers
11. _____ pine (state tree of 5-Across)
12. Canada's capital
13. Casino customer
18. Kick out
23. Straight, narrow cut
24. Ending with million or billion
25. The _____ State (North Dakota)
27. "_____ won't!" (firm refusal): 2 wds.
28. _____ Center (tourist attraction in Orlando, Florida)
31. _____ Arizona Memorial (tourist attraction in Honolulu, Hawaii)
32. _____ apso (small terrier)
33. Resident of Des Moines or Sioux City
34. Annoy
36. Lamb Chop puppeteer Lewis
41. Christianity or Hinduism: Abbr.
43. Big brass instrument
44. _____ all-time high: 2 wds.
46. Metallic element
49. Modifies formally
50. New_____ (Carlsbad Caverns locale)
51. Rough

52. "Drowning ___" (Bette Midler comedy of 2000)
56. Erie ___ (New York waterway)
59. California's Golden ___ Bridge
60. Having no depth or scope, for short: Hyph.
61. Highest point
63. ___ X'er (person born after 1965)
64. First state to join the Union: Abbr.
65. Positive vote
66. Surgery sites, for short
67. "___ too shabby!"

NATIVE AMERICAN HISTORY

ACROSS

1. South American Indian of old
5. Large pictures painted directly on walls
11. Egyptian boy-king
14. Unprejudiced
15. _____ Trail (route used during the U.S. westward migrations)
16. Unlock, in poetry
17. Opponent of General Custer in 1876: 2 wds.
19. Preschooler
20. "Bravo, bullfighter!"
21. Trick or _____
22. Former Attorney General Janet
23. Sticky stuff
24. Medicine man of certain Native American tribes
26. Long, easy stride
29. Female sheep
32. Place where tents are set up
33. Fragrance
35. Book of maps
37. Photo _____ (good opportunities for picture-taking)
40. "Wait just a _____!"
41. Battle of the Little _____ (conflict in which 17-Across defeated General Custer)
43. Permit
44. Come _____ screeching halt: 2 wds.
45. Indian _____ (large body of water)

46. "I'll Be _____" (Mariah Carey hit)
48. Possess
50. Ping-Pong partition
52. "The jig _____!" ("It's no use!"): 2 wds.
53. Native American buildings made from sun-dried brick
55. Finish
57. Catholic schoolteachers, often
58. Pace of a musical piece
61. Bic liquid
64. Sherlock Holmes's title: Abbr.
65. South Dakota village where 300 Oglala Sioux were massacred in 1890: 2 wds.
68. Greek letter between zeta and theta
69. Lure
70. Native American tribe that once inhabited the Great Lakes region
71. Urgent call for help
72. Neighbors of Kuwaitis, Iraqis and Jordanians
73. Cry out sharply, as a dog

DOWN

1. "Assuming that's true . . .": 2 wds.
2. A hammer may hit one
3. Give a speeding ticket to
4. Paintings, sculptures, etc.

5. President after Madison
6. Craving
7. Country star McEntire
8. Bust _____ (laugh uproariously): 2 wds.
9. "That's funny!", in a chat room
10. Long-running NBC variety show, for short
11. Carved, symbolic posts found at Native American dwellings: 2 wds.
12. "Once _____ time . . .": 2 wds.
13. Westernmost branch of the Dakota Indians
18. Judge of the Simpson trial
22. 29-Across's mate
23. Diamond, pearl or sapphire
24. "The Lion King" villain
25. "_____ he grown!" (phrase heard at a family reunion)
26. Custer's _____ stand (41-Across)
27. Black-and-white cookie
28. Native American woman who supposedly saved Captain John Smith
30. Minimum _____ (lowest legal pay rate)
31. Revolutionary Allen or actor Hawke

34. Higher than
36. "The _____ Ranger"
38. 1-Across's native country
39. Part of a flight of stairs
42. Puts the finishing touch on cake
47. Concealed
49. Tummy muscles
51. Cone-shaped Native American tents

53. Mountain range inhabited by the 1-Across
54. Because of: 2 wds.
56. Say "yes" with body language
58. Ballerina's skirt
59. Barenaked Ladies song from "Gordon"
60. 1,601 in Roman numerals
61. Concerning: 2 wds.

62. Tennant of the Pet Shop Boys
63. "_____ your fingers crossed!"
65. "Scream" director Craven
66. Out _____ limb (vulnerable): 2 wds.
67. Lock opener

1	2	3	4		5	6	7	8	9	10		11	12	13
14					15							16		
17				18								19		
20					21						22			
			23						24	25				
26	27	28			29	30	31		32					
33				34		35		36				37	38	39
40				41	42							43		
44				45					46	47				
		48	49				50		51		52			
53	54								55	56				
57					58	59	60				61	62	63	
64				65	66						67			
68				69							70			
71				72							73			

FAMOUS ARTISTS AND WORKS

ACROSS

1. Spanish Surrealist who painted "Persistence of Memory" [1904–89]
5. Frequent painting subject for French artist Edgar Degas [1834–1917]
10. "Not Tonight" rapper Lil' _____
13. Worshipped one
14. Site for a Wild West brawl
15. Historic time period
16. French Post-Impressionist who painted "The Card Players" [1839–1906]: 2 wds.
18. James Bond creator Fleming
19. Finished
20. Bus driver on "The Simpsons"
21. Mexican menu item
25. Dutch graphic artist who created optical illusions [1898–1972]: 3 wds.
29. Figurative illustration, as in paintings by 1-Across
31. Shrubby wasteland
32. Swampy stretch of land
33. Milky white gems
35. Circle segment
38. Abbr. in business names
39. Sustain with food
41. _____ Speedwagon (rock group)
42. Physician, for short
43. Feature of a dying fire
44. Tarzan's transport
45. Singer Marilyn or Lena
47. _____ glass (material that 23-Down worked with)
50. Words and drawings spray-painted in public places, used as an art form by 10-Down
53. Folk sayings
54. Capital of Latvia
55. "This is _____ pipe" (caption in René Magritte's painting "The Treachery of Images") 2 wds.
57. Eggs, to biologists
58. French painter who initiated impressionism [1840–1926]: 2 wds.
65. "Batman Forever" star Kilmer
66. More tightly packed
67. Element whose symbol is Fe
68. Right-angled building extension
69. Both _____ of the coin
70. "The _____ Supper" (painting by Renaissance man Leonardo da Vinci [1452–1519])

DOWN

1. Short swim
2. City southeast of Oklahoma City
3. "Mambo No. 5" singer Bega
4. Not feeling well
5. Stupefy
6. It may have a snooze button
7. _____ sequitur (statement with an illogical conclusion)
8. Person behind bars
9. 180° from WSW
10. American pop artist who used very simple figurative signs [1958–90]: 2 wds.
11. Hopping mad
12. Main house on an estate
14. Break off
17. Singer Natalie
20. Month before Nov.
21. Bashful
22. Essential _____ acids
23. Russian-born French artist whose paintings depicted Russian village life: 2 wds.
24. "When I was your _____ . . ."
26. Rocker and recliner
27. "Electric" fishes
28. Miss America's band
30. "Sure thing!": 2 wds.
34. Prefix with Raphaelite or Renaissance
36. "Jerry Maguire" co-star Zellweger
37. Female college students

39. Sponge ball producer
40. Prefix meaning "all"
44. By way of
46. Birds _____ feather: 2 wds.
48. Spud
49. Eve's partner
50. Spot for fruit trees
51. Adversary
52. Already occupied: 2 wds.
56. Praise-filled poems
58. Record store purchases
59. Waikiki neckwear
60. As well as
61. _____ colors (paint types)
62. Org. that supports firearms
63. Canon camera system
64. Blasting compound

1	2	3	4			5	6	7	8	9		10	11	12
13					14							15		
16				17								18		
				19							20			
21	22	23	24				25	26	27	28				
29					30		31							
32					33	34						35	36	37
38				39	40						41			
42				43						44				
		45	46					47	48	49				
50	51					52		53						
54						55	56							
57				58	59	60					61	62	63	64
65				66							67			
68				69							70			

AUTHORS AND LITERATURE

ACROSS

1. With 5-Across, Charlotte Brontë novel
5. See 1-Across
9. "_____ Frome" (Edith Wharton novel)
14. Missing from military service
15. First word of most letters
16. San _____, California
17. "The Adventures of Huckleberry Finn" author: 2 wds.
19. What knights' wives are called
20. Ambulance destinations: Abbr.
21. _____-Davidson motorcycle
23. Get out of bed
24. Use one's eyes
25. Sphere
26. "Cosmos" author Carl
28. Self-defense sport
29. Charles Dickens's "A Tale of _____ Cities"
30. Hair-styling goop
33. Dr. Seuss's "Horton Hears _____": 2 wds.
36. Cry noisily
38. Underground transportation
40. Bird bills
42. Sends a boxing opponent to the floor
44. "The Good Earth" novelist Buck
45. "1984" author George
47. Have unpaid bills
49. Use a keypad
50. "Are we there _____?"
51. Prepare to shoot a gun
53. Flows back, as the tide
55. _____ home run (does like Mark McGwire): 2 wds.
57. Female sheep
58. Chewing _____
61. Benjamin Franklin's "_____ Richard's Almanack"
63. Franklin who was known as "The Queen of Soul"
65. Genetic material
66. Talk show queen Winfrey
68. "The Grapes of Wrath" author John
70. "Inferno" author
71. 66-Across is one
72. Bundle of hay
73. Do what Rip Van Winkle did
74. Opening poker contribution
75. Suffix with prank, trick or gang

DOWN

1. "The Last of the Mohicans" author _____ Fenimore Cooper
2. Conscious
3. Greenland settlers of old
4. Antlered animal
5. Playwright Albee and poet Lear
6. Annual school publication
7. Train track component
8. With 11-Down, "A Farewell to Arms" author
9. "The Tonight Show" announcer Hall
10. Homecoming queen's headwear
11. See 8-Down
12. Gets older
13. Organ of smell
18. You, to Shakespeare
22. Swerves, as a ship
27. Ascend: 2 wds.
28. It has a punch line
31. Frontier sheriff Wyatt _____
32. Country singer Lovett
33. "_____ Named Charlie Brown": 2 wds.
34. Agatha Christie's "And Then There _____ None"
35. "The Scarlet Letter" author Nathaniel
37. Halloween shout
39. Puts money on it
41. Piece of a Venetian blind
43. Most sugary
46. Actress Bonet or Kudrow
48. "Charlotte's Web" author: 3 wds.
52. Actress Mason or Warfield
54. Lima _____
56. Very angry

ELECTRICITY AND MAGNETISM

ACROSS

1. It has a nucleus that electrons are bound to by electrical attraction
5. Cookbook feature
11. PC program, informally
14. First item to be filled out on most forms
15. Prolific inventor of electrical devices
16. Come _____ screeching halt: 2 wds.
17. Semiconductor devices that control the flow of current between two terminals
19. R.&B. trio with the hits "No Scrubs" and "Unpretty"
20. Walks pompously
21. Direction opposite WSW
22. Professional wrestler Hart
23. "What _____ to be the problem?"
25. Lacking sensitivity
26. "Attack, Fido!"
29. Circle segment
30. On _____ (without a client's commitment)
31. Hard as _____ : 2 wds.
33. Material of such low conductivity that the flow of current through it is negligible
38. "Drowning _____" (Bette Midler comedy)
39. _____ the sky (promise of future happiness): 2 wds.
40. Rock/soul singer Turner
41. Process by which a body with electric or magnetic properties produces magnetism or an electric charge in a neighboring body
43. Effect produced when electric current passes through the body
44. Federal meat-inspecting org.
45. "The Avengers" co-star Thurman
47. Hillary Clinton, _____ Rodham
48. Confronts
50. Take by force
52. _____ for (chooses)
53. What a spoilsport spoils
55. Pay increases
59. Rock's _____ Speedwagon
60. His experiments in electricity led him to invent the lightning rod: 2 wds.
62. Gas guzzler
63. Trying experience
64. New overseas currency
65. Ambulance destinations, briefly
66. Terminals by which current enters batteries
67. Sketched

DOWN

1. Aardvark's dinner
2. Like lemons
3. Actor Epps
4. Lists of options
5. "Mad About You" co-star Paul
6. Magazine workers: Abbr.
7. Quotes
8. "Help _____ the way!": 2 wds.
9. Tiny skin opening
10. Naval officer: Abbr.
11. Force that acts between oppositely charged bodies to draw them together
12. Regions of an electric battery or magnet that are in positive or negative states
13. Postwar agreements
18. T-bone, for one
22. Respiration
24. Caesar's 1,103
25. Klinger's rank on "M*A*S*H": Abbr.
26. _____-Am (Dr. Seuss character)
27. Metallic element with important magnetic properties
28. Substances through which electricity passes easily

30. Energy source of the solar system
32. Results in
34. Prefix with orthodox or liberal
35. Cranial cavity connected to the nasal passages
36. Formerly
37. Autumn lawn tool
39. School org.
42. Record store purchases
43. Plastic wrap material
46. Wall paintings
48. Electromagnetic ____ (interaction between electrically charged particles)
49. "... partridge in ____ tree": 2 wds.
50. Starving
51. Positioned the body into a V shape, as a diver
53. Nonflowering plant with fronds
54. Cancel
56. Pronounce indistinctly
57. Irish name of Ireland
58. December downfall
60. _____ constrictor
61. "Norma _____" (film for which Sally Field won Best Actress)

1 A	2	3	4	■	5	6	7	8	9	10	■	11	12	13
14 N	A	M	E	■	15						■	16		
17 T			18 S								■	19		
20 S			T	■	21			■		22				
■	■	23 S	E	24 E	M	S	■		25				■	■
26 S	27	28 C	■	29 A			■	30 S			■		36	37
31 A		O	32 K	■	33	34	35	U			36	37		
38 M		N	■	39			N	■	40					
41 I		P	42				■	43						
■	44 U			■		45	46		■	47				
48	49 C			■	50			■	51	■				
52 T			■	53 F	54	■	55			56	57	58		
59 O		■	60 E			61								
62 R		■	63 R			■	64							
65 S		■	66 N			■	67							

WOMEN'S HISTORY

ACROSS

1. Olympic gold medal winner Lipinski
5. Band draped around Miss America
9. _____ mater (school one graduated from)
13. Spoken out loud
14. Similar
15. Tree dropping
16. Chemist who discovered radium with her husband: 2 wds.
18. Poet Angelou
19. Pittsburgh football player
20. Former First Lady Roosevelt
22. Head movement that means "yes"
23. Felony involving fire
24. Tie fastener
27. Org. that collects income taxes
28. "Perfect 10" gymnast Comaneci
32. Cotton gin inventor Whitney
33. Actress Lanchester or hostess Maxwell
35. Go higher and higher, like 53-Across
36. Fathers
38. "Wuthering Heights" novelist Brontë
40. Potato, in slang
41. With 53-Across, first woman to fly across the Atlantic
43. Perform like Billie Holiday
45. Communist leader Mao _____-tung
46. Where Dr. Laura Schlessinger can be heard
47. Brother or sister, for short
48. _____ and aahed (expressed amazement)
50. "You're Still the One" singer Shania
52. Weary traveler's stopover
53. See 41-Across
56. Actress Bening or Funicello
60. _____ vera (skin lotion ingredient)
61. Nancy Kerrigan and Michelle Kwan: 2 wds.
63. Barbra Streisand, Helen Hunt or Madonna
64. Shoe bottoms
65. "Just you _____!"
66. Member of the Conservative Party in Great Britain
67. Thompson, Samms or Lazarus
68. Korbut of the 1972 Olympics

DOWN

1. "Uncle _____ Cabin" (Harriet Beecher Stowe classic)
2. "I smell _____!": 2 wds.
3. How some steaks are cooked
4. Extraterrestrials
5. Pronounce indistinctly
6. 53-Across's preferred mode of travel
7. Athletes like Picabo Street and Katja Seizinger
8. Shoe parts
9. Annually published fact books
10. What Jack Sprat's wife couldn't eat
11. BLT topping
12. Worship from _____
14. Scored 100% on
17. Run away and get married
21. Long, long time spans
23. "_____ in the Sun" (Lorraine Hansberry play): 2 wds.
24. Moth-repellent wood
25. Camel's South American cousin
26. Helped
27. Suffix with symbol or social
29. Swimming pool measurement
30. Occupied: 2 wds.
31. Used a plus sign
34. "Caroline in the City" actress Thompson
35. "Atlas Shrugged" author _____ Rand
37. Like a snake or an eel
39. Women's _____ (feminist movement)
42. Mamie Eisenhower's state of birth

#	Clue
44.	"_____ Fly Now" (theme from "Rocky")
47.	"Murphy Brown" or "Roseanne"
49.	"Testing, _____ three . . .": 2 wds.
51.	Get out of bed
52.	Fluids inside pens
53.	Where the sun rises
54.	Cher's voice range
55.	Lion's sound
56.	On the ocean
57.	Greenish blue
58.	High school math course, for short
59.	"¿Cómo _____ usted?" ("How are you?")
62.	Massachusetts state tree

20TH CENTURY INNOVATIONS

ACROSS

1. It connects a computer to the Internet [1958]
5. In the blink of _____: 2 wds.
11. Lifesaving technique performed in the E.R. [1960]
14. Have _____ to grind: 2 wds.
15. Credit _____ (Visa, American Express, etc.) [1950]
16. Boxing legend Muhammad
17. Record-store purchase: 2 wds. [1972]
19. Chemist's workplace
20. Taken temporarily, as a library book: 2 wds.
21. They may be IBM-compatible [1975]
22. _____ Aviv, Israel
25. Commandment violation
26. Keenly smart
29. Lifetime Achievement Award–winning director Kazan
31. Common antibiotic [1928]
34. Stylish Oldsmobile models
36. "Top _____ mornin' to you!": 2 wds.
37. "_____ Ventura: Pet Detective"
38. "Dawson's Creek" star James Van _____ Beek

39. School org.
40. Obtained
42. French for "one"
44. See 46-Across
46. With 44-Across, what a driver might shift into
49. Sugar substitute in diet soft drinks [1964]
52. Disney sci-fi film of 1982
53. Pacific and Atlantic
54. Color in the American flag
56. Site for a sauna and steambath
57. Kind of monitor screen for 21-Across: Abbr.
58. Touch-tone _____ (push-button innovations of 1964)
61. "Ready, _____, go!"
62. Car instrument that tells you how fast you're going [1902]
67. _____ Paulo, Brazil
68. Stick out like _____ thumb: 2 wds.
69. Last Greek letter
70. Make a mistake
71. Assembly _____ (piece-by-piece production systems) [1913]
72. Only U.S. President to resign

DOWN

1. Apple computer, for short [1984]
2. John Lennon's widow Yoko _____

3. Beaver's construction
4. Member of Montreal's baseball team
5. "This _____ war!"
6. First segment of a play: 2 wds.
7. Nothing, in Spain
8. "_____ go bragh!" ("Ireland forever!")
9. Units of three feet: Abbr.
10. Abbr. on a computer key
11. Hand-held devices that divide and multiply [1967]
12. Material that 15-Across are made of [1909]
13. Cut of meat that's often barbecued
18. Paper _____ (gizmos that hold sheets of paper together) [1900]
21. "The _____ Club" (Jim and Tammy Faye Bakker's former show)
22. _____ bag (pouch placed in boiling water) [1920]
23. 12th letter of the alphabet
24. Instrument used to help determine the truth: 2 wds. [1921]
26. German cry of dismay
27. Prolonged attack
28. Chemical suffix with ethyl or butyl

30. "_____ you for real?"
32. "The Hunchback of _____ Dame"
33. "Give _____ rest!": 2 wds.
35. _____ transplant (life-saving operation) [1958]
39. Fido's foot
41. Month before Nov.
42. Party card game
43. _____ reactor (radiation producer) [1942]

45. Suffix with host, heir or steward
46. _____ pad (dictation taker's need)
47. Letters between M and Q
48. Cloning material discovered in 1953
50. "Cool!"
51. Wears away gradually
55. Evil spirit
58. Lowly laborer

59. "_____ goes nothing!"
60. Eighteen-wheeler
61. Opposite of NNW
62. Actor Mineo or baseballer Bando
63. Letter before 69-Across
64. _____-Mex food
65. Self-love
66. Sprinted

MYTHOLOGY

ACROSS

1. Jet _____ (traveler's discomfort)
4. Father, informally: 2 wds.
10. The Argo of mythology, for example
14. "Double Fantasy" musician Yoko
15. Easter or Thanksgiving event
16. 43,560 square feet
17. Abode of the dead, ruled by Hades
19. Chinese lap dog, for short
20. Ruler after Night, in Greek mythology
21. 52, to Caesar
22. When the plane is due to land: Abbr.
23. Greek god of war
25. Mythological maze
29. Think about something constantly
32. Guarantee
33. "_____ for Lawless" (Sue Grafton novel): 2 wds.
34. Worldwide
38. One-time Russian ruler
39. Home of the greater Grecian gods: 2 wds.
41. Spanish for Bonkers
44. One who's panting
45. Sheep's sound
48. She was abducted by Zeus in the form of a bull
50. Take weapons away from
52. Ten-year conflict of mythology: 2 wds.
56. Play divisions
57. Realm of the god Apollo or Helios
58. Color
59. Pampering, for short
60. "How _____ to know?": 2 wds.
62. Leader of the Knights of the Round Table: 2 wds.
66. "The Shadow" star Baldwin
67. Eventually: 2 wds.
68. "Ode on a Grecian _____"
69. Miami-_____ (Florida county)
70. Nickname for a legendary Scottish lake monster
71. Realm of the god Neptune or Poseidon

DOWN

1. Olympic gymnast Mary _____ Retton
2. Advice columnist Landers
3. Isis, Aphrodite or Venus
4. Nashville's Grand Ole _____
5. Court TV topic
6. Amusing in an odd way
7. Human friend of Big Bird and Oscar the Grouch
8. Improvise: Hyph.
9. Homer Simpson's neighbor
10. Some Christians
11. Father of the river gods
12. Noah's 10-Across
13. Gadget that holds a golf ball
18. "_____ On Down the Road" (song from "The Wiz")
22. Suffix with north or northeast
23. Alternative to Prodigy or CompuServe
24. Baseball stat.
26. Cried out sharply, like a dog
27. _____ la la
28. That girl
30. "_____ Pepper's Lonely Hearts Club Band"
31. Advertiser's catch phrase
35. Suffix with schnozz
36. Fly-_____ (air show maneuvers)
37. Rock concert equipment
39. Milk, facetiously: 2 wds.
40. Geller with supposed mental powers
41. Allow
42. "And now a word from _____ sponsor"
43. Got to the other side of, like the river Styx
45. God of wine
46. Realm of Athena or Minerva
47. Grand _____ (sporty Pontiacs)

49. Greek god of forests and pastures
51. _____-N-Pepa (rap group)
53. Bellyache
54. Uncles' mates
55. Kathie Lee's co-host
59. One yielded golden apples in mythology
60. Lump of gum, for example
61. Chicken _____ king: 2 wds.
62. Blood relatives
63. "Who _____ to judge?": 2 wds.
64. Suffix with press or strict
65. Genetic material

THE HUMAN BODY

ACROSS

1. External ear parts
6. Funny bone's location
11. Vinyl records
14. It hangs from the soft palate at the back of the throat
15. "I _____ vacation!": 2 wds.
16. Shaggy ox of the Himalayas
17. Organ attached to the liver in which bile is stored
19. Roman 1,051
20. Antlered animal
21. Pale-green beans used in succotash
22. Stumble _____ (run across)
23. Tennis star Sampras
24. 100-yard _____
26. Direction opposite NNW
28. Bands of connective tissue
33. Fatty organic compounds in living cells
36. Pepsi, Coke or RC
37. _____ and aah
38. Punk/folk singer DiFranco
39. Eyeball parts that contain rods and cones
41. Female deer
42. Competed in a marathon
43. Yell "Heads up!" to

44. _____ of Langerhans (endocrine cell masses in the pancreas that secrete insulin)
46. Partition separating the thoracic cavity from the abdominal cavity
49. Wood used to make baseball bats
50. People born between July 23rd and August 22nd, astrologically
51. "Be that _____ may . . .": 2 wds.
54. "You only live _____"
56. They're between knees and ankles
58. Morning ABC show, for short
61. Communist leader _____ Tse-tung
62. Tiny blood vessels
65. Spring month: Abbr.
66. _____ Oyl (Popeye's love)
67. Major artery out of the heart
68. _____ blood cells
69. It makes up about 2/3 of the body's composition
70. Lower part of the large intestine

DOWN

1. Winter Olympics sledding event
2. Shape of the human face

3. _____ up (gain muscle mass)
4. Letter before em
5. Dark brown weasellike mammal
6. Hard covering of a 31-Down
7. _____ sheltered life (didn't experience hardships): 2 wds.
8. Snoozing sites
9. Praise-filled poem
10. Big battle
11. Glandlike tissue masses containing white blood cells: 2 wds.
12. _____ Alto, California
13. Essential component of the integumentary system
18. Illuminated
22. Take advantage of
23. Shar-_____ (Chinese fighting dog)
24. _____ Lama (religious leader)
25. Accumulate
26. Mount on which Moses was given the Ten Commandments
27. Length of nerve tissue extending down the back: 2 wds.
29. Cupcake covering
30. Qui-_____ Jinn ("The Phantom Menace" Jedi master)

31. Molar, incisor or cuspid
32. "_____ All That" (1999 romantic comedy)
33. Cooking fat
34. Time-traveling alien of British TV: 2 wds.
35. Alternative to J.C. Penney or Kmart
40. _____ la la
45. Back muscle, for short
47. _____ Wee Reese (baseball Hall-of-Famer)

48. Container for shipping merchandise
52. Long-running NBC variety show, for short
53. Sci-fi author Asimov
54. "The Mod Squad" co-star Epps
55. Back of the neck
56. It's produced by the salivary glands
57. Bee's home
58. "Two Guys and a _____" (ABC sitcom)

59. "Allow _____ introduce myself": 2 wds.
60. Strong _____ ox: 2 wds.
62. Mooing mammal
63. Chicken _____ king: 2 wds.
64. Winnie-the-Pooh's marsupial friend

1	2	3	4	5	■	6	7	8	9	10	■	11	12	13
14					■	15					■	16		
17				18							■	19		
20			■	21					■		22			
■			23				■		24	25			■	
■	26	27		■		28	29	30					31	32
33				34	35	■	36				■	37		
38			■	39		40				■		41		
42			■	43				■	44		45			
46			47				48	■			49			■
■		50				■		51	52	53			■	
54	55				■	56	57				■	58	59	60
61			■	62	63						64			
65			■	66					■	67				
68			■	69					■	70				

PEOPLE OF THE MILLENNIUM

ACROSS

1. Pioneering civil rights leader Parks [1913–]
5. Diana, Princess of _____ [1961–97]
10. Pa Clampett on "The Beverly Hillbillies"
13. "This is only _____ . . .": 2 wds.
15. "If _____ King of the Forest" ("The Wizard of Oz" tune): 2 wds.
16. Cheer for the bullfighter
17. "Romeo and Juliet" playwright [1550–1604]
19. Name of the computer in "2001: A Space Odyssey"
20. Egg-laying chicken
21. Grade between bee and dee
22. "The Divine Comedy" poet [1265–1321]
24. Actor, director and producer Chaplin [1889–1977]
28. "Haven't _____ you somewhere before?": 2 wds.
29. BB's and bullets
32. First American woman in space: 2 wds. [1951–]
34. Shrimp _____ (garlicky seafood dish)
37. Telegraphic code inventor Morse [1791–1872]
38. Title for 65-Across

39. Org. that approves toothpastes
41. "So's _____ old man!"
42. _____ la la (singing syllables)
45. "_____ Know What You Did Last Summer": 2 wds.
48. Detach, as a magazine page: 2 wds.
50. "Moonlight Sonata" composer [1770–1827]
53. Holocaust diarist _____ Frank [1929–45]; or Henry VIII's second wife _____ Boleyn [1507–36]
54. Ancient Peruvian, like those led by Atahualpa [c. 1500–33]
55. President who made the Bill of Rights part of the Constitution [1751–1836]
58. Snaillike garden pests
60. Suffix with velvet or Hallow
61. Three-time heavyweight champion Muhammad _____ [1942–]
64. Body part cut off by Vincent van Gogh [1853–90]
65. Law of gravitation formulator: 2 wds. [1642–1727]
70. 201, in Roman numerals

71. "Bonanza" star Greene
72. Bolívar who liberated five South American countries [1783–1830]
73. _____ shirt (casual top)
74. Olympic track-and-field star Jesse [1913–80]
75. Acquires

DOWN

1. Allergic reaction on the skin
2. "Top _____ mornin' to you!": 2 wds.
3. "Sweet and Lowdown" star Penn
4. Inquire
5. Windshield attachments
6. Feeling of amazement
7. "Caroline in the City" star Thompson
8. Make a mistake
9. It's found in an apple core
10. "Paradise Lost" poet: 2 wds. [1606–74]
11. Very happy
12. Computer key that erases letters
14. _____ support (help for computer users)
18. Vasco da Gama [c. 1460–1524] opened this type of route to the East Indies
23. Suffix with million or billion, as used for J. D. Rockefeller [1839–1937]

24. End of many Web addresses
25. _____ Vegas
26. "Now _____ me down to sleep . . .": 2 wds.
27. Fudd who tormented Bugs Bunny
29. Donkey
30. AT&T competitor
31. She and her husband discovered radium: 2 wds. [1867–1934]
33. _____ Gagarin (first person to make an orbital space flight) [1934–68]
35. Walkway
36. Expression like "in the doghouse" or "kick the bucket"
40. Prolific inventor Thomas _____ Edison [1847–1931]
43. Participate in a marathon
44. Chowed down
46. Adult male deer
47. _____ Zeppelin
49. Skillet
50. Cut in two
51. Intertwine, as strings of a tennis racket
52. Sister's daughters
56. Republic of China founder Sun Yat-_____ [1866–1925]
57. Dollar bills
59. Structure that may store fodder or missiles
61. "Don't look _____!": 2 wds.
62. Steal merchandise during a riot
63. Ramada, Sheraton and Holiday
66. Female pig
67. "_____ you sure?"
68. Raggedy _____
69. Hairpiece

1	2	3	4	■	5	6	7	8	9	■	10	11	12
13				14	15					■	16		
17				18						■	19		
20			■	21			■	■	22	23			
■	■		24			■	25	26	27	■	28		
29	30	31		■	32				33				
34			35	36	■	37					■	■	■
38		■	39		40		41			■	42	43	44
■	45	46				47		48		49			
50	51				52	■	■	53					
54			■	55			56	57		■	■	■	
58			59	■	■	60			■	61	62	63	
64		■	65	66	67	68			69				
70		■	71				■	72					
73		■	74				■	■	75				

THE MIDDLE AGES

ACROSS

1. Medieval slaves required to render services to a 6-Across
6. Manor owner of the Middle Ages
10. Angry crowd
13. Vast body of water
14. Computer users' correspondence: Hyph.
16. "You _____ what you eat"
17. Emperor of the Holy Roman Empire, 800–14
19. Acquire
20. Sent to the canvas, in boxing slang
21. President Reagan, for short
22. Forbidden things: Hyph.
24. Rotate
26. Coke or Pepsi
27. Person who easily becomes sentimental
30. School org.
32. Behaves
35. Pertaining to
36. French national heroine who ended the siege of Orléans in 1428: 3 wds.
38. Actor _____ Diamond Phillips
39. Medieval English poet who wrote "The Canterbury Tales"
41. _____ de Janeiro, Brazil
42. Shopkeepers who were common in the Middle Ages
44. Discourage
46. Pale in the face
47. "For _____ a jolly good fellow"
48. Ten-year period
49. Meat-grading org.
51. Cruel Roman emperor
52. "We _____ please!": 2 wds.
54. Bartender on "The Simpsons"
55. Sit-ups strengthen them
58. _____-Cone (icy treat)
59. Affliction that killed an estimated quarter of Europe's population in the 14th century: 2 wds.
64. Hundred Years' _____ (conflict between England and France, 1337–1453)
65. Stringed instrument of India
66. Grown-up
67. Naval officer: Abbr.
68. See 51-Down
69. St. Thomas Aquinas and St. Francis of Assisi, for example

DOWN

1. Footwear item
2. Reverberation
3. Enjoy a novel
4. _____ East (where Marco Polo traveled in the 13th and 14th centuries)
5. Weekend comedy series, for short
6. Sour fruit
7. Country west of the Arabian Sea
8. Dustcloth
9. Loud noise
10. Document of English liberties sealed in 1215: 2 wds.
11. Black-and-white cookie
12. Wagers
15. Joke-teller Jay
16. Fourth largest Great Lake
23. Norwegian king (1016–29) who became Norway's patron saint
24. Letters after R
25. Curve ball, for one
26. Walking stick
27. "Dogma" actress Hayek
28. Double-reed instruments
29. In medieval physiology, the elemental fluids blood, phlegm, black bile and yellow bile: 2 wds.
30. Sullen looks
31. Tic _____ (tiny breath mints)
33. Took a stab at
34. Make a touchdown, for example
36. "Sense and Sensibility" novelist Austen
37. "_____ in the court!"
40. "Very funny": 2 wds.

43. Abnormal sac
45. _____-friendly (safe for the environment)
48. Low-pitched, as a voice
50. Scooby-Doo, Benji and Pluto
51. With 68-Across, Gothic cathedral in Paris started in 1163
52. "It's the end of the world _____ know it!": 2 wds.
53. _____ instant (suddenly): 2 wds.
54. Polite thing to call a woman
55. "Son of _____!": 2 wds.
56. Gain muscle mass, with "up"
57. Goes down, as the sun
60. Get _____ of (throw away)
61. Seventh Greek letter
62. On the _____ (fleeing)
63. Commotion

INSECTS

ACROSS

1. Walking _____ (insect with a twiglike body)
6. Put _____ to (halt): 2 wds.
11. Toy dog, for short
14. Hammerin' Hank of baseball
15. Insect that hasn't yet undergone metamorphosis
16. Based _____ true story: 2 wds.
17. Insects found around bodies of water
19. Parking _____
20. Fall back, as the tide
21. Fourth month: Abbr.
22. Color of some 17-Across
23. Group whose members have high IQs
25. Bloodsucking insect that's a favorite food for 17-Across
27. _____-door neighbor
28. Get _____ of (throw away)
29. Large coffeepot
30. Eccentric comedian Philips
31. See 26-Down
33. Morning rush hour's end, approximately: 2 wds.
35. How-_____ (instruction manuals)
36. What "&" means
37. Lawyer's charge
38. Body part that can be stubbed
40. Take after Tara Lipinski
42. Map out
43. Sick
44. Jim's Big _____ (folk/pop band)
45. Green _____ Packers
46. Attend, as a party: 2 wds.
47. Groups of insects living together
50. Expresses pain vocally
52. Many-_____ (multicolored)
53. Ready to go
54. Bird that's a symbol of wisdom
55. "The Addams Family" cousin
56. 15-Across of a moth that spins a cocoon
61. Los del _____ ("Macarena" group)
62. What a shopper looks for
63. "There's _____ in sight" ("This could go on forever"): 2 wds.
64. Paper Mate product
65. People who frost cakes
66. Tiny biting insects

DOWN

1. Bummed out
2. Pothole-filling stuff
3. Paul's cousin on "Mad About You"
4. Convincing, as an argument
5. They're turned in order to open doors
6. 1980's sitcom featuring an alien
7. Deli meats
8. Three-legged camera stand
9. Once-_____ (quick examinations)
10. Mas' partners
11. 31-Across accomplish this as they go from flower to flower
12. From here _____ (as of now): 2 wds.
13. San _____ (city in west California)
18. Shaq's org.
22. Set fire to
23. Short office notes
24. Insect's hard outer covering
26. With 31-Across, prolific egg layers in hives
27. Insect-catching tool
28. With 59-Down, six-legged household pest
31. It's twirled in a parade
32. Direction opposite WSW
33. Chinese restaurant beverage
34. Sheds skin, as an insect
37. Insect that can follow "fruit," "butter" or "horse"
39. "Evil Woman" band, for short
41. "There is _____!": 2 wds.

42. Rabies vaccine developer Louis _____
45. Lightning bug or ladybug
46. Four quarts
47. Noise from a cricket
48. Protruding bellybutton
49. Singer Hayes who voices Chef on "South Park"
50. You may clean the floor with it
51. Having unpaid bills
56. 106, in Roman numerals
57. Hi-_____ monitor
58. "Caroline in the City" star Thompson
59. See 28-Down
60. Streets: Abbr.

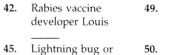

MUSIC

ACROSS

1. Michael Jackson's music category
4. Molars and canines
9. Org. for songwriters
14. Pat Benatar's "Love _____ Battlefield": 2 wds.
15. Conductor Previn or pianist Watts
16. Violin's larger relative
17. Portable wind instrument with a keyboard
19. "Do re mi fa so la ti do"
20. Intl. alliance with 16 member nations
21. Former lead singer of the Police
23. Use a couch
24. Filmmaker Welles
26. World _____ (baseball championship)
29. Overwhelming feeling of admiration
32. _____ Stones ("Ruby Tuesday" singers)
35. Do simple arithmetic
38. "Cornflake Girl" singer Amos
40. "Clueless" star Silverstone
41. Hawaiian necklaces
43. Church instrument
45. _____-N-Pepa
46. Lake _____ (site of the 1980 Olympics)
48. "_____ the Rainbow" ("The Wizard of Oz" tune)
50. Rocker David _____ Roth
51. "My Way" singer Frank
53. Swing _____ (time when big band music was popular)
54. Soak up
58. Trousers
61. Play by _____ (improvise)
63. High-strung, in slang
66. Anita Baker's music category
67. Andrew _____ Webber (73-Across composer)
70. Kenny G's instrument
72. Light beam in a CD player
73. Madonna movie musical
74. "_____ You Later, Alligator" (song by Bill Haley and the Comets)
75. "Carrie" star Spacek
76. Music symbols
77. Mind reader's gift

DOWN

1. Liberace's instrument
2. Songwriter Hammerstein (or the award he won in 1941 and 1946)
3. Postwar agreements
4. Cigarette ingredient
5. Terminates
6. Prepare for publication
7. French for "three"
8. "Taxi" star Marilu
9. Cooling systems: Abbr.
10. "Wait just a _____!"
11. Like Mozart's music
12. Sheryl Crow's "_____ Wanna Do": 2 wds.
13. Robert Frost or William Carlos Williams
18. Trisha Yearwood's "XXX's and _____'s"
22. Bad pun
25. _____ King Cole
27. Mariah Carey's "_____ Be There"
28. Yale students, informally
30. President Wilson
31. "To _____ is human . . ."
33. World's longest river
34. California's Golden _____ Bridge
35. Swiss mountains
36. Sandwich shop
37. Former lead singer of the Supremes
39. Billy Joel's "_____ to Extremes": 2 wds.
42. Sign of a healing wound
44. "_____ Maria" (popular wedding song)
47. "_____ My Party" (# 1 hit of 1963)
49. Queen Latifah's music category
52. Gotten out of bed
55. Shout after a rousing recital
57. Fire residue
58. Adjustable knot

1	2	3	■	4	5	6	7	8	■	9	10	11	12	13
14			■	15					■	16				
17			18						■	19				
20				■	21				22	■		23			
24				25	■		26			27	28			■
■			29	30	31	■	32	R	O	L	L	I	N	G
35	36	37	■	38			39	■	40					
41			42	■	43			44		■	45	S	A	L	T
46				47		■	48	O	V	E	R	■	50		
51					52	■	53				■	■	■	■	■
■		54				55	■			56	57	58	59	60
61 E	62 A	R	■	63			64	65	■	66				
67			68	69	■	70				71				
72				■	73				■	■	74			
75				■	76				■	■	77			

TALES OF MYSTERY AND SUSPENSE

ACROSS

1. "_____ for Murder" (1954 Alfred Hitchcock film): 2 wds.
6. The _____ Boys (fictional teenage sleuths)
11. Boxing win, for short
14. The word "Mississippi" has four of them
15. Talk show host Stewart
16. Concealed
17. Author of "The Firm" and "The Rainmaker": 2 wds.
19. Yale student
20. "Read _____ good books lately?"
21. _____-Magnons (Paleolithic humans)
22. Small land mass surrounded by water
23. When doubled, one of the Teletubbies
25. Hidden supply
28. Close but no _____
31. Person who works on crime cases
35. Got out of bed
36. Slip away from
37. Point of a pen
38. Mob scene
39. Greek letters after alphas
40. Puerto _____
41. Donkey
42. Knight's protection
43. Sherlock Holmes creator Arthur _____ Doyle
44. Best-seller by 17-Across made into a 1994 movie: 2 wds.
46. Furious
47. Worked clearing tables at a restaurant
48. "_____ of Steel" (workout video)
49. Hint that helps a 31-Across
51. Sick
53. Evansville's state: Abbr.
56. _____-pah-pah (tuba's sound)
57. J. K. Rowling's wizard-in-training: 2 wds.
62. Tear
63. Shady area formed by tree branches
64. Director Welles of suspense films
65. Suffix with steward or lion
66. R. L. _____, author of spooky stories for kids
67. Instrument with 88 keys

DOWN

1. _____ vu
2. "Help _____ the way!": 2 wds.
3. Pale, like someone reading 11-Down?
4. "Steal My Sunshine" band
5. Chinese food additive
6. It may be spiked or dyed
7. Too
8. Pep rally holler
9. Genetic molecule composition
10. Thanksgiving vegetable
11. 1980 film based on a Stephen King novel: 2 wds.
12. "A Time to _____" (best-seller by 17-Across)
13. "Garfield" dog
18. Producer of TVs and VCRs
22. Suffix with hobby or novel
23. "I Know What You Did _____ Summer" (novel by 50-Down)
24. "You _____ what you eat"
25. "_____ Little" (1999 film featuring a white mouse)
26. "Bill & _____ Excellent Adventure"
27. Card that beats a king
28. Jeweler's weight
29. St. Patrick's Day marchers
30. Series of stories by 66-Across
31. Considered
32. "Candle in the Wind" singer _____ John
33. Bishop's assistant
34. Wood used to make black keys of a 67-Across
39. White cheese produced in France
40. Director Howard and actor Silver

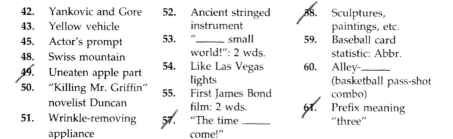

No.	Clue
42.	Yankovic and Gore
43.	Yellow vehicle
45.	Actor's prompt
48.	Swiss mountain
49.	Uneaten apple part
50.	"Killing Mr. Griffin" novelist Duncan
51.	Wrinkle-removing appliance
52.	Ancient stringed instrument
53.	"_____ small world!": 2 wds.
54.	Like Las Vegas lights
55.	First James Bond film: 2 wds.
57.	"The time _____ come!"
58.	Sculptures, paintings, etc.
59.	Baseball card statistic: Abbr.
60.	Alley-_____ (basketball pass-shot combo)
61.	Prefix meaning "three"

Grid answers (handwritten):

- 1-Across: D E J A ...
- 6-Across: HARDY
- 11/13: O
- 16: HID
- 19: I
- 20: A
- 21: CRO
- 22: ISLE
- 23/24: LA
- 25: STAΣH
- AR
- TECT
- SE
- ELUDE
- T
- AS
- R
- CONAN
- T
- 49: C
- 56: O
- 57: HARRY POTTER
- 62: R
- 63: AR
- 65: ESS
- 66: STINE
- 67: PIANO

WEATHER

ACROSS

1. Small balls of falling ice
5. "_____ luck!" ("Break a leg!")
10. They're worth 6 pts. in football
13. _____ Olay (brand of face cream): 2 wds.
15. Fighting intensely: 2 wds.
16. Significant stretch of time
17. Fall to the earth's surface as condensed water
19. Actor Gibson or director Brooks
20. President Lincoln, for short
21. "Fifth Beatle" Yoko _____
22. N.B.A. coach Riley
23. Month before Nov.
26. Diner sandwich
28. Blew suddenly and strongly, as the wind
31. "Hot enough _____ You?"
32. She lived in the Garden of Eden
33. Clinton investigator Kenneth
34. Heavy rainfall may cause this
37. Toronto Maple _____ (N.H.L. team)
40. What you might say after spilling something

41. Falls to the ground in flakes
44. "Who'll _____ the Rain" (Creedence Clearwater Revival song)
45. It may cover the ground on a cold morning
47. Atmospheric _____ (weather statistic)
49. Prolonged attack
52. Devoured
53. Competitor of Panasonic, Sony and JVC
54. Unlocked
55. School org.
56. "Yikes, a mouse!"
57. "Be quiet!"
58. Give the thumbs-down to
60. Mind reader's ability
62. Actress West of old films
63. Science dealing with the weather and climate
68. Hockey Hall-of-Famer Bobby
69. Where sports events are held
70. Queen Amidala's home planet in "The Phantom Menace"
71. "_____ whiz!"
72. Doppler _____ (storm detection system)
73. El _____ (Pacific current responsible for weather upheaval)

DOWN

1. Move like a rabbit
2. It gets polluted by 57-Down
3. French for "Island"
4. Ricky Martin's "Livin' La Vida _____"
5. Chou En-_____ (former Communist leader)
6. Bart Simpson's bus driver
7. Sharp sounds produced by a banjo
8. Warmed the bench: 2 wds.
9. "What _____ you afraid of?"
10. How cold or hot it is outside
11. Fear greatly
12. It's sprinkled on icy roads
14. Told a little white lie
18. Where your hipbones are
23. "Get _____ My Cloud" (Rolling Stones hit): 2 wds.
24. Rainbow feature
25. Zone 6–12 miles above the Earth where weather conditions manifest themselves
27. Its capital is Nashville: Abbr.
29. Actor Mineo or baseballer Maglie
30. Lock of hair
35. "Doctor Dolittle" actor Davis

36. What Republicans are known as, for short
38. Hurricane-_____ winds
39. "_____ for yourself!"
42. Prepare a gift
43. Irish _____ (dog breed)
46. Perfect gymnastics score
48. Hurricane _____ (annual period when hurricanes develop)
50. Parts of scientific names that come before species
51. Prepared for publication
54. Chicago airport
57. Hazy atmospheric pollution
59. "Warrior Princess" of TV
61. Arrange in advance
63. Tarnish
64. Rowboat mover
65. _____-Wan Kenobi
66. Geometrical suffix with penta-, octa- or poly-
67. "_____-hoo!"

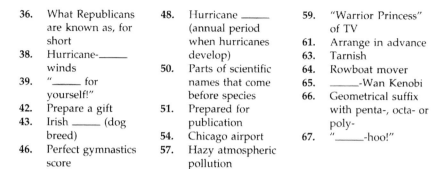

BLACK HISTORY MONTH

ACROSS

1. Civil rights heroine Parks
5. Droops
9. Cooling device
12. Milky white gem
13. Horse's pace
14. "The Color Purple" author Walker
16. Host of "Kids Say the Darndest Things": 2 wds.
18. Insects that eat clothes
19. "On your mark, get _____, go!"
20. Missing, like a soldier
21. Makes you say "Wow!"
22. "Fame" star _____ Cara
23. Where Charles Rangel and Maxine Waters serve: Abbr.
24. _____ the Grouch
27. Sight in the night sky
29. 1-Across wouldn't give up hers
32. Relating to sound
34. Hit with a sci-fi gun
36. _____ de Janeiro, Brazil
37. Competed like Jesse Owens
38. Important time period
40. Suffix with Japan or Vietnam
41. Popular place for a tattoo
42. Dog's bark
43. The "D" of "C.D." or "D.J."
45. _____ Renaissance (period of black literary renewal)
47. Give careful attention to
49. Hit the mall
51. _____ bear (stuffed animal)
52. Do, _____, fa, so, la, ti, do: 2 wds.
54. "Rudolph the Red-_____ Reindeer"
56. Musical dramas
58. Identical brother or sister
59. Foot part
62. Hopeless one
63. Slave who was the subject of a 19th-century Supreme Court case: 2 wds.
65. 45-Across leader Alain _____
66. Acting part for Will Smith, for example
67. Textbook division
68. Before, in poetry
69. With 9-Down, jazz singer known as the "Queen of Scat"
70. Leaning Tower of _____

DOWN

1. Burglarizes
2. Boy in "The Andy Griffith Show"
3. Pepper's partner
4. Sheryl Crow's "_____ I Wanna Do"
5. "Uncle Tom's Cabin" author Harriet Beecher _____
6. Crimes involving fire
7. Fancy drinking glasses
8. Pig's place
9. See 69-Across
10. Stomach discomfort
11. Loch _____ Monster
14. Bullets and BB's
15. Bank offerings
17. Lugged
21. Had _____ on (was very fond of): 2 wds.
22. Author Fleming or actor McKellen
24. Talk-show queen Winfrey
25. Not be stingy with
26. Southern Christian Leadership _____ (Martin Luther King Jr.'s organization)
28. Had breakfast
30. Shown on television
31. "Men in Black" star _____ Lee Jones
33. Emergency situation
35. Tidies up
39. Bonfire remnant
44. Remote _____ (television accessory)
46. Fire engine's color
48. Actress Bo
50. Former Joint Chiefs of Staff chairman Colin _____
53. Female horse
55. Part of the record containing the hit song, usually: 2 wds.
56. Make eyes at
57. Penniless

59. "Beloved" novelist Morrison

60. "The Adventures of Milo and _____" (1989 family film)

61. Soul singer _____ James

63. Rapper Dr. _____

64. Half a pint

1	2	3	4		5	6	7	8				9	10	11
12					13					14	15			
16				17						18				
19					20				21					
			22						23					
24	25	26				27		28			29		30	31
32					33		34			35		36		
37				38		39		40				41		
42				43			44		45		46			
47			48		49			50		51				
		52		53			54		55					
56	57						58					59	60	61
62					63					64				
65					66					67				
68					69					70				

U.S. PRESIDENTS

ACROSS

1. He ended the era of reconstruction by taking the last federal troops out of the South (#19, 1877–81)
6. Under him, California and the New Mexico Territory were won in the Mexican War (#11, 1845–49)
10. It comes before Feb.
13. Counting everyone: 2 wds.
14. Cheek makeup
15. "Who _____ kidding?": 2 wds.
16. He created the U.S. Department of Education (#39, 1977–81): 2 wds.
18. Blend
19. Choose by ballot, as a president
20. Late-night host Jay
21. "_____ were the days!"
24. His victory in an Indian battle led to his campaign slogan "Tippecanoe and Tyler Too" (#9, 1841)
27. Benedict Arnold was one
29. Ship's steering apparatus
30. 16-Across's middle name
31. On a cruise: 2 wds.
34. Baseball Hall-of-Famer Mel
37. It fills a football
38. Lincoln who delivered the Gettysburg address (#16, 1861–65)
40. "Bill _____, The Science Guy"
41. Hog's home
42. Eleanor Roosevelt, to Theodore Roosevelt
43. Web addresses
44. Mary _____ Lincoln (38-Across's wife)
46. Wild Australian dogs
49. He was assassinated after four months in office (#20, 1881)
53. "I've Grown Accustomed _____ Face" (song from "My Fair Lady"): 2 wds.
54. Share a border with
55. Shoot for: 2 wds.
57. What President Jefferson might have been called by friends
58. He appointed the first female Attorney General and the first female Secretary of State (#42, 1993–2001): 2 wds.
64. Actress Gabor or Argentine political figure Perón
65. "Now that's what _____ service!": 2 wds.
66. "_____ get to the fun part!": 2 wds.
67. Title of some politicians: Abbr.
68. What the second "N" of CNN stands for
69. He directed the strategy that successfully concluded the Civil War (#18, 1869–77)

DOWN

1. Letters after G
2. "Not a Pretty Girl" singer DiFranco
3. Sweet potato
4. Freddy Krueger's street
5. Most crafty
6. Covered area leading to a doorway
7. "I'm _____ here!" ("Later!")
8. Size bigger than medium: Abbr.
9. Prefix with flop or plunk
10. Under him, the Missouri Compromise was passed (#5, 1817–25): 2 wds.
11. Essential _____ acids
12. He resigned as a result of the Watergate scandal (#37, 1969–74).
14. "The Facts of Life" star Charlotte
17. Mark Antony's love, for short
20. Rapper _____ Kim
21. Characteristic
22. He initiated a policy to provide aid to countries threatened by Communism (#33, 1945–53): 2 wds.
23. Engine additive
25. "Cheers" actress Perlman
26. 500 sheets of paper
27. Beverages containing caffeine
28. Opposite of well-done, in a restaurant

32. Tic-_____-toe
33. Storage place for tools
35. He was the first vice president to become president upon the death of the chief executive (#10, 1841–45)
36. Della's role on "Touched by an Angel"
38. "Jimmy crack corn, _____ don't care . . .": 2 wds.
39. _____ one's time (wait for a good opportunity)
43. "Disgusting!"
45. Frequently, to poets
47. Language spoken in Rome: Abbr.
48. Observing carefully
49. Microsoft billionaire Bill
50. Higher than
51. 1986–94 NBC legal drama: 2 wds.
52. Pickles that aren't sweet
56. Caesar's 1,150
58. Recycling receptacle
59. Water at 31°F
60. Neither here _____ there
61. US Airways alternative
62. "Mind your _____ business!"
63. Volleyball partition

THE ROARING TWENTIES

ACROSS

1. Jazz _____ (period from 1918 to 1929, roughly)
4. Its capital is Washington, D.C.
7. Letters between S and W
10. "Touched by an Angel" network
13. Rock star Stewart
14. Nickname of jazz trumpeter Louis Armstrong, who gained popularity in the 1920's
16. Chart-topping song, like Al Jolson's "Sonny Boy" in 1928
17. Nickname of a 1925 court case in which John Scopes was charged with teaching evolution in the classroom: 2 wds.
19. Long _____ (way back when)
20. Stretch across
21. Negative votes
22. Zodiac sign
24. "_____ the ramparts we watched . . ."
27. Illegal liquor, as that produced and smuggled during 68-Across
29. Golfer who, from 1922–30, won 4 U.S. Opens, 5 U.S. Amateurs, and 3 British Opens: 2 wds.
34. "What _____ you thinking?"
35. Prefix with cycle or sex
36. Fourth-largest Great Lake
37. The Roaring 20's and the Gay 90's, for example
39. Bluegrass instrument
41. Person who favors the banning of alcoholic drinks, as during 68-Across
43. Member of Houston's baseball team
46. TV detective Peter or "Treasure Island" character Ben
48. "_____, vidi, vici" (Caesar's declaration)
50. Acorn-dropping tree
51. Kindergartners recite them
53. Warren G. Harding and Calvin Coolidge, in the 1920's
56. Feed and protect, as offspring
58. Quiet _____ mouse: 2 wds.
59. Respond to a bad pun
60. 1,105, in Roman numerals
63. Sing without backup
67. Naval officer: Abbr.
68. Period (1920–33) when the 18th Amendment was in force and alcoholic beverages were banned
72. Give a massage to
73. Month in 1929 when the stock market crashed
74. How an on-line chatter says "That's funny!"
75. Austin Powers is one
76. _____-Bo (exercise system)
77. U-turn from WSW
78. Airplane's place

DOWN

1. "A Farewell to _____" (1929 Ernest Hemingway novel)
2. Sticky stuff
3. Novelist Ferber who wrote "So Big" (1924) and "Show Boat" (1929)
4. "_____ only as directed"
5. Utter
6. Abbr. on the bottom of an envelope
7. "Let _____ a lesson!": 2 wds.
8. "Sweet and Lowdown" actress Thurman
9. Swedish-made car
10. Lively ballroom dance of the 1920's
11. More sizable
12. Moe, Larry or Curly
15. _____-Magnon (Paleolithic population of humans)
18. Door fixture
23. "_____ a dark and stormy night . . .": 2 wds.
25. Keep an _____ (watch): 2 wds.
26. _____ Nabisco (one of the 100 largest U.S. companies)
28. Suffix of sugars
29. Slangy address for a man
30. End _____ sour note: 2 wds.
31. Legendary crooning singer whose career began in the late 1920's: 2 wds.

32. Suffix with human or planet
33. Fiber that conducts impulses from the spinal cord
38. Sudden attacks, as on saloons selling alcohol illegally during 68-Across
40. "_____ Gigolo" (31-Down hit): 2 wds.
42. "_____ Sir! That's My Baby" (hit song of 1925)
44. It may get its dinner from a dumpster
45. Gives the go-ahead to

47. Radio station that broadcasts "All Things Considered" and "Car Talk": Abbr.
49. MTV hostess Peeples
51. Infuriates
52. Be infuriated: 2 wds.
54. Couch potato's clicker
55. In 1924 the _____ Coast first heard a radio broadcast from the British Isles
57. Take out of its container, as a houseplant

61. Margaret of stand-up comedy
62. Feeling you get about someone, informally
64. Lubricates
65. "_____ Homeward, Angel" (1929 Thomas Wolfe novel)
66. The "O" of "R.O.M."
69. Alternative to JVC or Panasonic
70. "_____-Hur" (1926 film based on a Lew Wallace novel)
71. Its capital is Dublin: Abbr.

1	2	3		4	5	6		7	8	9		10	11	12
13				14			15					16		
17			18									19		
20						21				22	23			
			24	25	26			27	28					
29	30	31				32	33				34			
35				36					37	38				
39			40			41		42		43			44	45
		46			47		48		49			50		
51	52				53	54				55				
56			57					58						
59					60	61	62			63	64	65	66	
67			68	69				70	71					
72			73								74			
75			76				77				78			

BIODIVERSITY

ACROSS

1. Hidden supply
6. Angry response to a come-on
10. Farm animal that gives milk
14. Playful, web-footed swimmer
15. Feature of a rooster's head
16. Govern
17. Huge, thick-skinned African animal
19. Giant panda's continent
20. Butterfly catcher
21. Yankee Doodle's mount
22. Late-blooming flower
23. Rabbit's refuge
24. Homes for 60-Across
26. Begin to grow, as a plant
29. Ferocious felines
33. "What's the ____?"
34. Moved on ice
35. Shape of a horse's racecourse
36. Tennis shoe feature
37. On all ____ (how a 10-Across walks)
38. Freshwater food fish
39. Disgusting
40. With 22-Down, predatory insect that travels in vast swarms
41. ____ for (chose)
42. Prickly plants with purple flower heads
44. Works the dough
45. Web addresses, familiarly
46. Animal with antlers
47. Ornate, like a peacock's tail
50. After-bath powder
51. Even if, for short
54. Stink like a skunk
55. Tree-hammering bird
58. Spoken
59. "____ Lang Syne"
60. Jungle roarers
61. Pierce through, as with a bull's 1-Down
62. Easter flower
63. Rope to catch an 18-Down

DOWN

1. Bony, projecting growth on a 10-Across
2. Will-____-wisp (delusion): 2 wds.
3. Busily working: 2 wds.
4. Stimpy's canine companion
5. One who doesn't finish high school
6. ____ of the crime
7. Brightly-colored parrot
8. "Te ____" ("I love you" in Mexico)
9. "Sesame Street" network
10. Jumping insect
11. Remove from office
12. "I cannot tell ____": 2 wds.
13. Rip
18. Male foal
22. See 40-Across
23. Shrub yielding fragrant, yellow tubular flowers
24. Milk farm
25. Concludes
26. ____-pea soup
27. Capture wild animals illegally
28. Talk show host Lake
29. Dark purple fruits
30. Madonna musical set in Argentina
31. Gathered leaves in a pile
32. Some huskies pull them
34. Painful places
37. Season when squirrels gather nuts
41. Composition of an amoeba or paramecium: 2 wds.
43. Attempt
44. Large seaweed
46. ____-longlegs (spider look-alike)
47. Tadpole, eventually
48. Flight: Prefix
49. Close to
50. Highway tax
51. Boxing wins, for short
52. Roosters' mates
53. "... ____ it would seem": 2 wds.
55. ____-Mart
56. Yes, in France
57. U.S. espionage org.

NATIONAL POETRY MONTH

ACROSS

1. "My _____ Duchess" (Robert Browning poem)
5. Self-esteem
8. Game show host
13. "Woe is me!"
14. Like a snail or a turtle
15. Gets close to
16. "Because I could Not Stop for Death" poet Emily
18. "William Shakespeare's Romeo & Juliet" co-star Claire
19. "The People, _____" (Carl Sandburg work)
20. Took to court
21. "Say it _____ so!"
22. Use a shovel
23. "The Snow _____" (Wallace Stevens poem)
25. What a student studies for
28. Something of value
31. Poet Henry _____ Longfellow
33. Congratulatory strokes on the back
34. Capital of Colorado
35. "There has to _____ better way!": 2 wds.
36. 3, on old clocks
37. _____ alai (game similar to handball)
38. Like slippery winter roads
39. "Ode on a Grecian _____" (poem by 59-Across)

40. Letter between kay and em
41. Slap handcuffs on
43. "Star _____: The Next Generation"
44. "Rime of the Ancient Mariner" poet Samuel Taylor _____
46. Toys on strings
47. "_____ go bragh!" ("Ireland forever!")
48. Eggy Christmas drink
49. Shakespeare's "Shall I Compare Thee to a Summer's _____?"
50. Sounded like a bell
52. Picnic spoiler
54. Greek letter before omega
57. Like the numbers 2, 3, 5, 7 and 11
59. "Ode to a Nightingale" poet: 2 wds.
61. Makes less severe
62. Butter substitute
63. "One Fish Two Fish Red Fish _____ Fish" (Dr. Seuss book)
64. Removes the skin from, like an apple
65. "Nightmare on _____ Street"
66. Old Mother Hubbard couldn't find one

DOWN

1. "The _____ of Shalott" (Alfred Lord Tennyson poem)

2. "I cannot tell _____": 2 wds.
3. Pouchlike structures in the body
4. "Shame on you!"
5. "So what _____ is new?"
6. "Roseanne" actor John
7. "Mind your _____ business!"
8. Comes to a finish
9. "I didn't _____ !" ("It was an accident!"): 2 wds.
10. "The _____ Tales" (Geoffrey Chaucer work)
11. Before, in poetry
12. Suffix with host or lion
14. "_____ as a bug in a rug"
17. "_____ really true?": 2 wds.
21. Bee, ant or grasshopper
22. _____ Moines, Iowa
24. Give recommendations to
26. Sound system
27. "I appreciate it!"
28. Each
29. Popeye, for one
30. Maya Angelou poem: 3 wds.
31. Oddball
32. Like Seinfeld's humor
34. Like a stuntman's deeds
37. Cookie container
42. Appetizer at a Chinese restaurant: 2 wds.

43. Creation of Santa's elves
45. Tooth covering
46. Pull quickly and forcefully
49. Fred Flintstone's pet
51. Loch _____ Monster
53. Throat sound used as an attention-getter
54. _____ Alto, California
55. Leave awestruck
56. "That makes sense": 2 wds.
57. _____ rally (school event)
58. Actress _____ Dawn Chong
59. "Home Alone" actor Pesci
60. Flow back, as the tide

1	2	3	4		5	6	7		8	9	10	11	12
13				14				15				
16			17				18					
19			20				21					
		22			23	24		25		26	27	
28	29	30		31			32					
33			34					35				
36		37			38			39				
40		41		42			43					
44		45				46						
47			48			49						
	50	51		52	53			54	55	56		
57	58			59			60					
61				62			63					
64				65			66					

AFRICA

ACROSS

1. It covers the summit of 10-Down
5. Bite between meals
10. South African word for "hill" that sounds like a police officer
13. Commotion: Hyph.
14. Shrivel, as a dying flower
16. Intense anger
17. African country that was formerly a British colony and protectorate: 2 wds.
19. Place for balm or gloss
20. Capital of the African country Togo
21. Small-statured natives of equatorial Africa
23. Cape _____ (African country consisting of a group of islands in the Atlantic)
26. Health club
27. Prefix meaning "both"
28. Greek vowels
29. Pottery material
31. Hits
32. Prefix with cycle or angle
33. Sailor's cry
34. "Do you have two fives for _____?" 2 wds.
35. African country that's an independent member of the French Community
37. Commercial capital of the Ivory Coast
40. "Family _____" (game show)
41. South African of Dutch descent
42. Convenience store clerk on "The Simpsons"
43. Have a big crush on
45. "Beverly Hills, 90210" actor Perry
46. Difficult journey
47. Dress worn by Hindu women
48. Wooden nail
49. Selected
50. Endangered African cat that's the fastest land animal
52. Flower holder
54. The word "lullaby" has three
55. African country that was formerly called Upper Volta: 2 wds.
60. _____-picker (overly critical one)
61. Shirt part that can be rolled up
62. African cat with a mane
63. Karl Marx's "_____ Kapital"
64. Symbol on a one-way sign
65. Large coffeepots

DOWN

1. They cross aves.
2. "_____ won't!" (firm refusal): 2 wds.
3. Poem of praise
4. Planets
5. Dog-paddled, for example
6. African river that flows through Cairo, Egypt
7. Had a 5-Across
8. Forming irregular, broken waves, as the sea
9. African country that's a member of the Commonwealth of Nations
10. Volcanic mountain in Tanzania that's the highest peak in Africa
11. Familiarize with new surroundings
12. Some colas
15. Rule: Abbr.
18. _____ v. Wade
22. Did a lawn chore
23. Docs for dachshunds
24. To be, in France
25. African regions of tall, densely growing evergreens: 2 wds.
26. Utter
29. African country that's a member of the French Community
30. Chat-room chuckle
31. Mix
33. Chills and fever caused by malaria, a disease that's reemerging in Africa
34. Busy as _____: 2 wds.
36. Creepy

37. Astronaut's affirmative: Hyph.
38. Chimpanzees, gorillas and other African primates
39. Atomic bomb, for one
41. The deadly African tsetse fly, for example
43. Go up, as a plane
44. Popular ball-shaped flower
45. Bush-Gore debate moderator Jim
46. Sickness often caught in winter: 2 wds.
48. Cole or Abdul of pop
49. Group of 11 Southern states that seceded in 1860–61: Abbr.
51. Atlanta-based "Superstation"
52. In _____ (occurring within an organism)
53. All over again
56. Prefix with plop or plunk
57. Smog pollutes it
58. Father's Day gift giver
59. Slip-_____ (easy-to-get-into shoes)

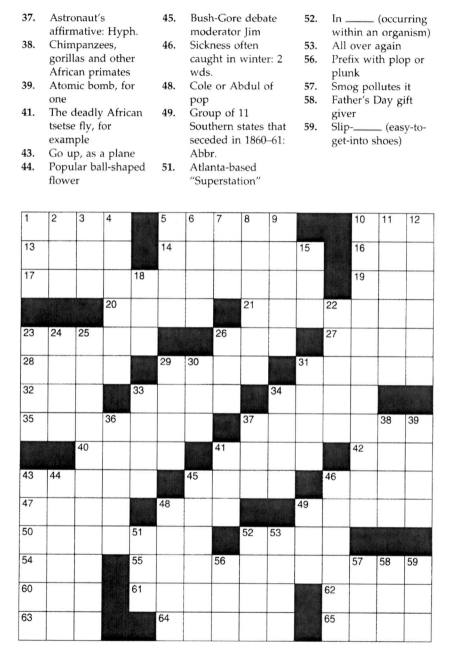

LONGITUDE & LATITUDE

ACROSS

1. Nevada city near Lake Tahoe [39.31 N, 119.48 W]
5. Shania Twain's "____ This Moment On"
9. Persian Gulf country [22.00 N, 58.00 E]
13. Russian river [47.00 N, 51.48 E]
14. City near Sacramento [38.07 N, 121. 16 W]
15. "Is that ____?" ("Really?"): 2 wds.
16. It flows through Cairo, Egypt: 2 wds. [30.10 N, 31.06 E]
18. ____ Pole [90 S, 0.00]
19. Chinese restaurant beverage
20. Opposite of WSW
21. ____-of-the-moment (without advance notice)
22. Blasting stuff
23. One of the Great Lakes [48.00 N, 88.00 W]
27. Three-time U.S. Open winner Hale ____
30. "Let's eat!": 2 wds.
31. One of Cher's friends on "Clueless"
32. Taunton ____ (city in southwest England) [51.01 N, 3.06 W]
33. Its capital is Teheran [35.40 N, 51.26 E]
34. Sound from the dog pound
35. Actors Asner and Harris
36. Pouchlike part
38. "Bill ____, The Science Guy"
40. Nothing
41. Fire residue
42. Robin or cardinal
44. Neighbor of New Hampshire [45.15 N, 69.15 W]
46. Hawaiian necklace
47. Christopher Columbus's birthplace [44.25 N, 8.57 E]
48. Boasts
49. Home of the Padres and Chargers: 2 wds. [32.42 N, 117.09 W]
51. ____ Lanka [7.00 N, 81.00 E]
52. Polite fellow
53. "Yippee!"
54. Attorney's org.
57. British goodbyes
59. Iowa's capital: 2 wds. [41.36 N, 93.36 W]
62. Island of 51-Down [13.55 S, 171.45 W]
63. Black-and-white cookie
64. Actress Loughlin or Petty
65. ____ out of shape (flustered)
66. Gold-medal figure skater Lipinski
67. Sicilian resort city [37.34 N, 14.16 E]

DOWN

1. Littlest of the litter
2. Pennsylvania port [42.07 N, 80.05 W]
3. Simba's mate in "The Lion King"
4. "Bravo, bullfighter!"
5. Michigan city [43.00 N, 83.41 W]
6. Wander
7. Praiseful poem
8. Russian space station
9. "Days ____ Lives" (soap opera): 2 wds.
10. West African country [20.00 N, 12.00 W]
11. Play a part
12. To the ____ degree
15. Colorado ski resort city [39.11 N, 106.49 W]
17. City in northwest France [48.05 N, 1.41 W]
21. Like a porcupine
22. Element #50
23. How to address a sergeant
24. Neighbor of Kenya [1.00 N, 32.00 E]
25. Rowing a boat
26. Weapons of war
27. Standards of perfection
28. Waters west of Saudi Arabia: 2 wds. [20.00 N, 38.00 E]
29. The Evergreen State [47.30 N, 120.30 W]
30. Cutting into cubes
37. Red as ____: 2 wds.

39. Human's earliest life stage
43. Quintana _____ (Mexican state) [19.40 N, 88.30 W]
45. Actress Meyers of "Kate & Allie"
47. Japanese knife of TV commercials
50. Handed out cards
51. Island group near Fiji [14.00 S, 171.00 W]
53. River of France and Belgium [51.09 N, 2.43 E]
54. Abbr. used when the author is unknown
55. Capital of Switzerland [46.57 N, 7.26 E]
56. 33-Across's continent [50.00 N, 100.00 E]
57. Rubber ducky's home
58. Jungle swinger
59. On the _____ (exactly)
60. Chapter in history
61. _____ de France [49.00 N, 2.20 E]

1	2	3	4	■	5	6	7	8	■	9	10	11	12
13				■	14				15				
16			17				18						
19			■	20			■	21			■		
■		22			■	23	24				25	26	
27	28	29		■	30				■	31			
32			■	33			■		34				
35		■	36	37		■	38	39		40			
41		■	42		43		■	44	45				
46		47				■	48						
49		50			■	51			■				
■	52			■	53			■	54	55	56		
57	58			■	59	60			61				
62			■	63				■	64				
65			■	66				■	67				

NUTRITION

ACROSS

1. Pertaining to milk, cream, butter or cheese
6. Shopper's delight
10. Take advantage of
13. Submit right before the deadline: 2 wds.
15. Video game or Disney sci-fi film of the 1980's
16. Holiday drink made with 12-Down
17. Triangle-shaped chart that shows federal dietary guidelines: 2 wds.
19. Droop
20. Interior design
21. Carbohydrates such as glucose, fructose and lactose
23. Abbr. on a Monopoly board
25. Roman 1,400
27. Cooking container
28. Fragrances
31. Chop down
33. Cluster of small feathers
36. Chicken or lamb serving
37. Massage
39. Unit used to express the energy value of food
41. Gobbled up
42. Prefix meaning "equal"
43. From _____ Z (completely): 2 wds.
44. "Honest" president
45. Substance essential to normal metabolism, as thiamine or niacin
47. "_____ sher!" ("Like, definitely!")
48. Perfect diving score
49. Swindle
50. Suffix with Hallow or velvet
52. People that take the bus, for example
54. One who may count to 48-Across in a boxing match
56. "So _____ me!"
58. Doorkeepers may need to check them
59. Direct a smile toward: 2 wds.
62. Weight loss queen Jenny _____
65. "Interview With the Vampire" actor Stephen
66. Compound found in animal-based foods that can clog arteries
71. Advice columnist Landers
72. "_____ a chill pill!"
73. Sweet baked food made of dough
74. Jan., Feb., Mar., etc.
75. "Yes, yes!", in Spain
76. Shock jock Howard

DOWN

1. Rock's _____ Leppard
2. Shakespeare's "Much _____ About Nothing"
3. "Where do _____ from here?": 2 wds.
4. Become flushed, as cheeks
5. Exclamation of fright or surprise
6. White, tasteless carbohydrate that's an important constituent of rice and potatoes
7. Elbow locale
8. "Superman" reporter Lane
9. Finish: 2 wds.
10. Kind of fat that's heart-healthy
11. Fly like an eagle
12. Breakfast items that are high in 66-Across
14. Where the Empire State Building is: Abbr.
18. CD-_____ (PC insert)
22. Attend: 2 wds.
23. _____ acid (essential constituent of vinegar)
24. People who do not eat meat, fish or fowl
26. Nonstimulating coffee
28. People from Serbia, Poland and Croatia
29. Quick haircut
30. "Wake Up Little _____" (Everly Brothers hit)
32. Nutritionists recommend drinking eight glasses of this every day

<table>
<tr><td>34.</td><td>Foods containing a high amount of plant carbohydrates, such as whole grains and fruits</td></tr>
<tr><td>35.</td><td>Most MTV watchers</td></tr>
<tr><td>38.</td><td>Body parts that are strengthened by calcium</td></tr>
<tr><td>40.</td><td>"Tank Girl" star Petty</td></tr>
<tr><td>46.</td><td>Last word of a prayer</td></tr>
<tr><td>51.</td><td>Atom centers</td></tr>
<tr><td>53.</td><td>What the body will do to consumed food</td></tr>
<tr><td>55.</td><td>Nutrition _____ (listing of ingredients that is required by law to be printed on food packages)</td></tr>
<tr><td>57.</td><td>Before, in poetry</td></tr>
<tr><td>59.</td><td>Unit of dietary fat</td></tr>
<tr><td>60.</td><td>Former Attorney General Janet</td></tr>
<tr><td>61.</td><td>Resident of Bangkok</td></tr>
<tr><td>63.</td><td>Egyptian cobra</td></tr>
<tr><td>64.</td><td>"Take _____ a compliment!": 2 wds.</td></tr>
<tr><td>67.</td><td>Gives the go-ahead to</td></tr>
<tr><td>68.</td><td>Numbered highway: Abbr.</td></tr>
<tr><td>69.</td><td>Hockey Hall-of-Famer Bobby</td></tr>
<tr><td>70.</td><td>"She's All That" actress Jodi _____ O'Keefe</td></tr>
</table>

1	2	3	4	5		6	7	8	9		10	11	12
13				14		15					16		
17				18							19		
		20					21		22				
	23	24				25		26		27			
28			29	30		31		32		33		34	35
36			37		38		39		40				
41			42				43				44		
45		46				47				48			
49				50		51		52		53			
	54		55		56		57			58			
59	60			61		62		63	64				
65				66		67					68	69	70
71				72					73				
74				75						76			

PAGE ONE

ACROSS

1. Box to the left of the 60-Across that contains the newspaper's slogan
4. Puts on the brakes
9. _____ strip (feature of the 23-Down)
14. Before, in poetry
15. Hoops superstar Shaquille
16. Soap _____ (daytime TV show)
17. Most important news article on the front page: 2 wds.
19. Removes the skin from, as an apple
20. Sorrow
21. Printed name of a news article's writer
22. Not difficult
23. Number of quarts in a gallon
25. Bill's partner in an "excellent adventure"
26. Mess up
28. Newspaper label that highlights longer articles in a series
30. Team trainer
33. Direction from N.Y.C. to Boston: Abbr.
34. General meaning
37. Song form the 50's, for example
38. Shania Twain's "_____ Man of Mine"
39. President between Grant and Garfield
41. "Cómo _____ usted?" (Spanish 101 phrase)
42. Tell a whopper
43. The Lone Ranger's pal
44. Made corrections to newspaper articles, for example
46. Mountain _____ (soft drink brand)
47. School org.
50. Deposits, as eggs
51. Resident of Bangkok
54. Not taken out, like passages of a newspaper article: 2 wds.
56. Menus list them
59. Group that may call a newspaper strike, for example
60. Newspaper's designed title
62. _____ code (communication system)
63. Have a big crush on
64. 2,000 pounds
65. Freedom of the _____ (right to publish freely)
66. The human body has 206
67. Finish

DOWN

1. "Electric" fishes
2. _____ code (part of a telephone number)
3. Brief paid messages at the bottom of newspaper columns: 2 wds.
4. They get hooked up to fire hydrants
5. Unable to sit still
6. People born between July 23rd and August 22nd
7. Black paving material
8. Like a fox
9. What the © on the front page stands for
10. October birthstone
11. Kind of badge earned by a Boy Scout
12. "Fame" star _____ Cara
13. Enclosed in a box
18. Genetic material
21. Prickly plant part that sticks to clothing
23. Newspaper section with cartoons
24. Followed orders
26. Prefix that means "environment"
27. Jack Dawson or Romeo, to Leonardo DiCaprio
28. Century 21 employee's area of expertise
29. "See ya later!"
31. Quote
32. Quick summaries of newspaper articles' contents
35. Agency that buys and distributes various newspaper features
36. French for "head"
40. Female pig
45. Actor McKellen or Ziering
47. Roly-poly

48.	Luciano Pavarotti is one
49.	In flames
51.	"_____ has to be a better way!"
52.	Expectations
53.	Feel crummy
55.	Throw
56.	"Let's go!"
57.	Prince William's school
58.	E-mail command
60.	Catch, as a criminal
61.	Shakespeare's "Much _____ About Nothing"

1	2	3		4	5	6	7	8		9	10	11	12	13
14				15						16				
17			18							19				
20								21						
		22					23	24				25		
26	27				28					29				
30			31	32	33				34			35	36	
37					38				39					40
	41				42				43					
		44		45								46		
47	48	49		50					51	52	53			
54			55				56					57	58	
59					60	61								
62					63						64			
65					66						67			

CHINA

ACROSS

1. Capital of the People's Republic of China
8. _____ Biao (Chinese marshal and Communist leader)
11. Pop's partner
14. Teacher who may help a student choose courses
15. Greek vowel
16. Santa _____, California
17. Endangered Chinese mammals: 2 wds.
19. "_____ the land of the free . . ."
20. Hang _____ Index (major Hong Kong stock market index)
21. With 76-Across, Chinese political and revolutionary leader Sun _____
22. Playful prank
24. Boat paddle
27. Flower holder
29. "This _____ sudden!": 2 wds.
30. "Now hold on a _____!"
33. Mechanical memorization
35. First-class: Hyph.
37. "Well, _____-di-dah!"
38. _____ and aah
39. Native of an administrative division of China that's the world's highest country

42. "Patience _____ virtue": 2 wds.
43. Do something with
44. Fitting
45. Neighbor of Mex. and Can.
46. In Chinese history, the Sung (960–1279), Ming (1368–1644) or Manchu (1644–1912)
48. Chinese-American "Charlie's Angels" co-star Lucy
49. Chill in the air
50. Merriment
51. Egg-laying chickens
52. It's pumped into a car
53. _____ California (narrow Mexican peninsula)
55. Baseball card stat
57. Document earned by a high school dropout, for short
59. Get out of bed
61. Classifieds and personals
63. Helper: Abbr.
67. East China _____ (part of the Pacific Ocean)
68. Lightly flooded grain-growing fields common in China: 2 wds.
72. Bed-and-breakfast
73. From _____ Z: 2 wds.
74. Lipton product: 2 wds.
75. Pester
76. See 21-Across

77. Holiday that, in China, is represented by one of 12 animals: 2 wds.

DOWN

1. Sacks
2. Singer Adams or Brickell
3. Tennis star Lendl
4. Person who professes patriotism loudly and excessively
5. Suffix with violin or guitar
6. Letters before Q
7. Middle-ager's hair color, often
8. Resulted in: 2 wds.
9. "Give _____ rest!": 2 wds.
10. Rocket-launching org.
11. Chairman of the Chinese Communist party, 1943–76: 2 wds.
12. "No _____ to blame": 2 wds.
13. _____ Polo (Venetian traveler who made journeys to China)
18. Back of the neck
23. Three times three
25. Stir up
26. Year of the _____ (1957, 1969 and 1993, in the Chinese calendar)
28. _____ Rebellion (attempt to overthrow the Manchus, 1850–64)

1	2	3	4	5	6	7		8	9	10		11	12	13
14								15				16		
17						18						19		
20						21				22	23			
			24	25	26		27		28		29			
30	31	32		33		34			35	36				
37				38				39					40	41
42				43				44				45		
46			47					48				49		
		50				51						52		
53	54			55	56			57		58				
59			60		61		62			63	64	65	66	
67			68	69			70	71						
72			73			74								
75			76			77								

PLACES AND REGIONS

ACROSS

1. Characteristic of the country
6. Boot-shaped European country
11. Mas' partners
14. Singing syllables: 2 wds.
15. City on the Alabama River
16. PC key near "Ctrl"
17. Surrounding things, conditions or influences
19. U.S. organization that gathers facts about other countries' governments
20. Direction from San Francisco to Los Angeles: Abbr.
21. _____ bomb on (overwhelm with surprising news): 2 wds.
22. Examine closely, as evidence
23. "Catch you later!"
24. Fixed service charge: 2 wds.
27. São _____ and Príncipe (west African country)
30. Ticked off
33. Actor Morales
34. Forgets to include
36. Administrative divisions of Canada
40. "Neato!"
41. Islands of the central and south Pacific, collectively
43. Cheerleader's yell
44. Country consisting of 13,677 islands in the Malay Archipelago
46. Clamor
48. Animal known as "the king of the jungle"
49. Direction 180° from 20-Across: Abbr.
51. City north of Des Moines
52. Last grade in high school
55. Inquire
57. Small deer with three-pointed antlers
58. Island of Western Samoa
61. Paintings and sculptures, for example
64. Historic time period
65. Plants of a wooded area: 2 wds.
68. Suffix with 48-Across that means "female"
69. On _____ (having continued good luck): 2 wds.
70. 820-mile European river
71. Stage scenery
72. _____ Domingo (capital of the Dominican Republic)
73. County in southeast England

DOWN

1. Numbered highways: Abbr.
2. Large coffeepots
3. Wild dance party
4. Boxing great Muhammad
5. Full of cooking fat
6. "This _____ time for jokes!": 2 wds.
7. Short-term staff member
8. Shake like _____: 2 wds.
9. Letters after K
10. Sun _____-sen (Chinese revolutionary leader)
11. Ocean edge that is the locale of Hong Kong, Thailand, Japan, etc.: 2 wds.
12. "_____ Less Ordinary" (Ewan McGregor/Cameron Diaz comedy): 2 wds.
13. Division of the United States, Mexico or India
18. City in north central Utah
22. Friend of Eric, Kyle and Kenny on "South Park"
23. Wager
25. Strauss of jeans fame
26. Like many countries of the 11-Down
27. "Beverly Hills, 90210" actress Spelling
28. Nation of the 29-Down whose capital is Muscat

29. Area from Libya east to Afghanistan: 2 wds.
31. Primatologists study them
32. A plumber may unclog it
35. "_____ a gun!": 2 wds.
37. "Take _____ empty stomach": 2 wds.
38. Make less severe
39. "_____ All That" (1999 teen flick)
42. Hundredth of a dollar

45. Squeak-stopping liquid
47. Acorn producer
50. Animator Disney
52. Major components of a 65-Across
53. From bad to _____
54. One of the Great Lakes
56. Capital of Bolivia
59. Animal skin
60. Capital of Norway
61. Car rental company that "tries harder"

62. "The Adventures of Rocky and Bullwinkle" actress Russo
63. "Jurassic Park" dinosaur, for short: 2 wds.
65. Musical notes between mi's and sols
66. "... man _____ mouse?": 2 wds.
67. Exclamations of surprise

1	2	3	4	5	■	6	7	8	9	10	■	11	12	13
14					■	15					■	16		
17				18							■	19		
20			■	21					■		22			
■		23			■		24	25	26				■	
27	28	29		■	30	31	32	■	33				■	
34			35	■	36		37					38	39	
40		■	41	42						■	43			
44		45					■	46	47					
■	48				■	49		50	■	51				
52	53				54	■	55	56			■			
57			■	58	59	60			■	61	62	63		
64		■	65	66					67					
68		■	69				■	70						
71		■	72				■	73						

IMMIGRATION

ACROSS

1. Passport endorsement allowing entry into a foreign country
5. Locale of Pier 21, a waterfront shed in Halifax that was once an important immigration entry point
11. Nourished
14. Frankenstein's humpbacked helper
15. National _____ (immigrants birth country)
16. Bullfight cheer
17. New York Harbor locale that was once an important immigration entry point: 2 wds.
19. _____ Tin Tin (heroic dog of 1950's TV)
20. "_____ is me!"
21. Plants that are used in skin creams
22. Vegetables in pods
23. "Help!", to a sailor
24. A dozen minus two
25. "Seinfeld" character
27. Bummed out
28. Losing color, as a frightened person's face
30. Church instrument
33. An immigrant permanently changes this
36. German socialist Marx
37. Light _____ feather: 2 wds.
38. Element whose symbol is Pb
39. Place where many immigrants work at low wages, for long hours, and under poor conditions
42. Brand of breath mints
43. Raise from the surface, as letters on a wedding invitation
44. "You never _____ it so good!"
46. Kind of labor often done by immigrant workers
47. "Kapow!"
48. U.S.S.R. secret police
51. Circle segments
52. Where an immigrant's ship lands
54. Pie _____ mode: 2 wds.
55. Genetic material
56. Like immigrants that have been officially granted the rights and privileges of citizenship
59. "_____ Force One" (1997 Harrison Ford film)
60. Natives of a foreign country who have not been 56-Across
61. Transportation for oceangoing immigrants
62. Media mogul Turner
63. Song parts that usually precede choruses
64. Sickness also known as "kissing disease"

DOWN

1. Looks at
2. House made of ice
3. Foot parts
4. "Kate & Allie" actress Meyers
5. Arranged in spirals
6. Felony involving fire
7. It flows through Cairo, Egypt
8. "What _____!" ("This is so much fun!"): 2 wds.
9. Loud noise
10. Alien _____ Sedition Acts (1798 laws empowering the president to expel dangerous aliens)
11. Person native to another country
12. _____ Gonzalez (child refuge at the center of a custody battle between the U.S. and Cuba)
13. Tightly packed
18. The Devil
22. Having wood siding
25. Cotton-gin inventor Whitney
26. Eye coverer
27. Deli meats
28. Coins that a Mexican immigrant might try to exchange
29. "Pronto!", for short
30. Gives the go-ahead to

31. "Monday Night _____" (wrestling show)
32. Immigrant's work permit: 2 wds.
33. Pep rally cheers
34. Purring pet
35. People who work on magazines: Abbr.
40. "Exact broadcast time not yet known": Abbr.
41. Note between fa and la
42. Llama's cousin
44. Pester
45. Quite annoyed with: 2 wds.
46. Bert's buddy
47. Carried, as a burden
48. Musical toy that's blown into
49. Discover little by little
50. Go from _____ worse: 2 wds.
52. Rouse from sleep
53. Colors
56. Pertaining to one of the armed forces: Abbr.
57. Ginger _____
58. Huge computer company

THE CIVIL WAR

ACROSS

1. "Battle Hymn of ___ Republic" (song written by Julia Ward Howe during the Civil War)
4. Jack, king and queen
9. Org. that approves and bans substances
12. 1996 presidential candidate H. ___ Perot
14. One who became 73-Across when 36-Across issued the Emancipation Proclamation in 1863
15. Quarter or penny
16. With 69-Across, landmark in central Virginia where the Civil War ended
18. Pull along slowly
19. High-IQ organization
20. "___ the ramparts we watched . . ."
21. What "General" was to 75-Across or 29-Down
22. ". . . man ___ mouse?": 2 wds.
24. Prince ___ (Aladdin's alter ego)
26. Do, re, mi, fa, ___, la, ti, do
27. "___ American Cousin" (play that 36-Across was watching when John Wilkes Booth assassinated him)

30. Creek in Georgia that was the scene of a Confederate victory in 1863
34. At the summit of
36. Lincoln who was president during the Civil War
37. Fishhook attachment
38. Picture puzzle
40. Computer that isn't produced by 31-Down
42. Students take them in class
45. "___ Brockovich" (Julia Roberts film)
47. Sticky stuff in tree trunks
49. ___ Virginia (state created in 1863 when some residents of Virginia didn't want to secede)
50. What 29-Down did to 75-Across at 16-Across on April 9, 1865
54. 36-Across's political party: Abbr.
55. Colonizing insect
56. "___ whiz!"
57. Furry foot
59. Actor Martin or quarterback Young
61. Abbr. used when the exact air time isn't known
64. Long couches
68. Storage structure on a farm
69. See 16-Across
71. Adam and Eve's first home

72. ___ a limb (in a dangerous situation): 2 wds.
73. No longer in bondage
74. Bottled hair coloring
75. Civil War Union general who later became president of the United States
76. Shaggy ox

DOWN

1. London streetcar
2. Expectation
3. "X-Games" cable channel
4. Group of 11 Southern states that seceded from the U.S. in 1860–61: Abbr.
5. Female choir member
6. Assign a "PG-13" to, for example
7. "New World Symphony" composer Antonin
8. Male or female
9. South Carolina landmark whose bombardment by the Confederates began the Civil War on April 12, 1861: 2 wds.
10. Conversation
11. "Mrs. Santa Claus" star Lansbury
13. Neither wonderful nor terrible
15. 401, in Roman numerals

17. "I Need to Know" singer _____ Anthony
21. Simba's friend in "The Lion King"
23. "I caught you!"
25. Statute
27. Rowboat mover
28. Sport-_____ (off-road vehicle)
29. Confederate general in the Civil War: 3 wds.
31. Huge computer corporation
32. _____-fire (truce)
33. In _____ (single file): 2 wds.
35. Copy a contented cat
39. Prolonged attack
41. Auto
43. Suffix with Siam or Japan
44. Motor oil additive
46. U-turn from SSW
48. Liveliness
50. Mouthed off to
51. Messy
52. Roundabout route
53. It's longer than a hyphen
58. Barking sound
60. "Snow Falling on Cedars" actor Max _____ Sydow
62. Dr. Dre's "Nuthin' _____ 'G' Thang": 2 wds.
63. Elvis _____ Presley
65. Intense anger
66. On the ocean
67. Look for
69. Gear tooth
70. Blasting stuff

ANIMAL LIFE CYCLES

ACROSS

1. Insect that hasn't yet undergone metamorphosis
6. Stylish
10. Suffix with manner or mystic
13. Constellation between Pisces and Taurus
14. Letters between K and P
15. "_____ and the King" (1999 Jodie Foster film)
16. Periods when an animal is developing in the womb
18. "Shoo!"
19. Opposite of NNW
20. Newborn dogs
21. Fully developed, as an animal
23. Cut of meat that's often barbecued
24. Couch that turns into a sleeper: 2 wds.
25. "Hamlet" star Hawke
28. Crow's cry
30. Tax-deferred savings: Abbr.
31. .035 ounce, in the metric system
32. Tijuana Brass trumpeter Herb
34. Darken in the sun
37. Gumption
38. Insects in the transformation stage between 1-Across and imago

39. Ingredient in some vinegars
40. "Wait just a _____!"
41. They make a clown look very tall
42. Ages and ages
43. Actor Linden or Holbrook
45. Video game console introduced in 1985, for short
46. "The Balcony" painter Édouard _____
47. Shedding feathers or skin, as some animals do while developing
50. Marino or Aykroyd
51. Recording label of Sarah McLachlan and Whitney Houston
52. Bathtub buildup
54. Place for a jacuzzi
57. "The Adventures of Rocky and Bullwinkle" actress Russo
58. Substances released by animals that influence other members of the same species
61. Garment for Caesar
62. "I'm so hungry I could _____ horse!": 2 wds.
63. Animal that is 21-Across
64. Snake's sound
65. Male deer
66. Without a _____ stand on: 2 wds.

DOWN

1. Falls behind
2. Greek war god
3. Go up
4. Animal doctor
5. Neat _____ (very tidy): 3 wds.
6. Film fragment
7. Medical insurance plans, for short
8. Motel
9. "Seinfeld" character _____ Kramer
10. Process of sitting on 25-Down while waiting for 27-Down to emerge
11. Entrap, as an animal
12. Paired up for the purpose of breeding
15. "When You Wish Upon _____": 2 wds.
17. Bathing fixture
22. Throw _____ (rant): 2 wds.
23. Male sheep
24. Workout clothes
25. They develop in ovaries
26. Not false
27. Birds, reptiles or fish that have recently come out of 25-Down
28. Giving a hint to
29. Cider flavor
32. Likely
33. Second scale degrees
35. "Vittorio the Vampire" novelist Rice
36. Where a newborn bird is raised

39.	No longer allow to suckle	47.	Trading centers	54.	Tight-fitting
41.	Narrow cut	48.	Cream-filled cookies	55.	Animal skin
44.	On the ocean: 2 wds.	49.	Backs of necks	56.	Concerning: 2 wds.
46.	Animal that gives birth to live young	50.	Twosome	59.	Sombrero, for one
		52.	_____ new standard: 2 wds.	60.	Praise-filled poem
		53.	Steep, rugged rock		

THE AMERICAN REVOLUTION

ACROSS

1. "The _____-Spangled Banner"
5. _____ of Liberty (Stamp Act opposers of 1765)
9. "I tought I taw a puddy _____!"
12. Water-transporting tube
13. Refuse: 2 wds.
14. Enter the water headfirst
15. American Revolution soldier who led the Green Mountain Boys: 2 wds.
17. It may leak from a battery
18. Dollar division
19. American Revolution general Benedict who became a traitor in 1780
21. Almanac contents
24. Female horse
26. Negative vote
27. Judge who presided over the Simpson trial
28. Roomy car
31. What a weightlifter shows off, for short
33. Notes between do and fa: 2 wds.
35. "Sanford and Son" star Foxx
36. Where sports teams play
39. America's "Uncle" and others
40. In flames
42. Very dry, as a desert
43. Cave-dwelling dwarf of folklore
45. _____-friendly software
46. Ricky Martin's "Livin' La Vida _____"
47. Keanu's role in "The Matrix"
48. Planted seeds
50. Precious stone
51. Urgent call for help
53. Sign of the future
55. Seven _____ War (1756–63 war won by England and Prussia)
57. _____ of Paris (1783 agreement that ended the American Revolution)
59. Make _____ (wager): 2 wds.
61. "You _____ seen nothin' yet!"
62. Site of the first major battle of the American Revolution in 1775: 2 wds.
68. Finish in last place
69. She sang "Tomorrow" and "Dumb Dog"
70. One of the Great Lakes
71. Chemical suffix with ethyl or butyl
72. Upside-_____
73. Tardy

DOWN

1. "Murder, _____ Wrote"
2. Preschooler
3. Barbecue residue
4. Respond
5. _____-N-Pepa (rap group)
6. Olive _____ ("Popeye" girl)
7. Direction from Providence to Boston: Abbr.
8. Submarine-detecting device
9. Fort captured by 15-Across in 1775
10. Theresa of _____ (sainted Spanish nun)
11. Stuffed bear named after President Roosevelt
13. _____ Francisco
14. Roseanne's TV hubby
16. Loch _____ Monster
20. Country star McEntire
21. _____ Continental Congress (American Revolution group in session in 1774)
22. "Don't shed _____ for me": 2 wds.
23. 1776 Thomas Paine pamphlet that supported the idea of an American Revolution: 2 wds.
24. Second Continental Congress member who later became the 4th U.S. President

25. War of 1812 hero Jackson who later became the 7th U.S. President
29. Chapter in history
30. Make harmless, as a bomb
32. Spoken
34. Gilligan was stranded on one
37. More friendly
38. American Revolution leader John or Samuel

41. Before, in poetry
44. Steal goods during a riot
49. One who changes hair color, for example
51. Like week-old bread
52. Constellation known as "the Hunter"
54. "Oops, I goofed": 2 wds.
56. Lucy's best friend on "I Love Lucy"
58. Scarfed down

59. Similar (to)
60. Honeycomb resident
63. Party card game
64. Direction 45° from 7-Down: Abbr.
65. Paul's cousin on "Mad About You"
66. Ignited
67. Pamela Anderson __

1	2	3	4		5	6	7	8		9	10	11
12					13					14		
15				16						17		
			18					19	20			
21	22	23				24	25			26		
27				28	29	30			31	32		
33			34		35				36		37	38
39					40			41		42		
43				44		45				46		
		47				48			49		50	
51	52			53	54				55	56		
57			58				59	60				
61				62	63	64				65	66	67
68				69						70		
71				72						73		

ARCHAEOLOGY

ACROSS

1. Archaeologists use these to locate dig sites
5. Docking places for boats
11. Flow back, as the tide
14. Make _____ (wager): 2 wds.
15. _____ borealis (northern lights)
16. VI x II
17. Egyptian boy-king whose tomb was unearthed by Howard Carter in 1922
19. Comedian Bill, for short
20. Foot part
21. Nectar-collecting insect
22. Hair on a lion's neck
23. Kind of badge earned by a boy scout
26. Bulgarian, Czech or Serbian
28. Establishes as law
30. Object found at an archaeological dig
32. Grassy ground surface that an archaeologist might have to dig through
33. Go one better than
35. Hole in the ground created by an archaeological dig

36. Locale of Harappa, Pakistan, where archaeologists have unearthed buildings from a complex ancient society
38. Sonnet writers, for example
40. Helps
43. College south of Toledo: Abbr.
45. Fertile area in a desert
47. Alley-_____ (pass-shot combo in basketball)
48. Material poured into 11-Down when digs are completed
51. Marathon participant
53. Teen idol singer/actor Frankie of the late 1950's
54. Opposite of a macho man
55. Italian coins
56. Carpenter's cutter
59. "Murder, _____ Wrote"
60. Place where a 30-Across may be scientifically analyzed
61. Peruvian city of the ancient Incas discovered by archaeologist Hiram Bingham in 1911: 2 wds.
66. From _____ Z (completely): 2 wds.

67. Opening at which fluid enters
68. Geologic time periods that are understood more fully by archaeological discoveries
69. Cub scout unit
70. Gave an examination to
71. "_____ people never learn!"

DOWN

1. Doorstep item that may say "welcome"
2. Monkey in "Aladdin"
3. House animal
4. Word before electricity or cling
5. Stop sleeping
6. "What'd you say?"
7. Persian Gulf resident
8. Italian capital whose ancient ruins have been studied by archaeologists
9. Most liberated
10. _____ Lorenzo (ancient Olmec center studied by archaeologists)
11. Holes dug by archaeologists to search for or expose buried items
12. Like the Six Million Dollar Man
13. Cut in half
18. "_____ worry!" ("Never fear!"): 2 wds.

22. Secretive organized crime group
23. Small plateau
24. Baseball Hall-of-Famer Slaughter
25. _____ dating (method of determining the age of an organic object)
27. Balm or gloss may be applied to it
29. Eat dinner
30. "Have I got _____ for you!": 2 wds.
31. Decays
34. Archaeologists trowel, for example
37. It's between the foot and the leg
39. Title for archaeologist Flinders Petrie or Leonard Woolley
41. "_____ that answer your question?"
42. Quick on one's feet
44. Saucer in the sky
46. Japanese fish dish
48. Sentimental song
49. Operate an airplane
50. Bonkers
52. Nephews' sisters
57. Plays a role
58. "I beg your pardon?"
59. Went like lightning
61. Cambridge college that offers degrees in archaeology: Abbr.
62. Hawaiian guitar, for short
63. _____-Magnon man (early Homo sapiens whose remains were first found in France in 1868)
64. Club sandwich ingredient
65. Avail oneself of

1	2	3	4		5	6	7	8	9	10		11	12	13
14					15							16		
17				18								19		
			20				21				22			
23	24	25							26	27				
28				29			30	31						
32			33		34				35					
36			37		38			39		40		41	42	
		43		44		45			46		47			
48	49			50			51		52					
53								54						
55				56	57	58		59						
60			61			62				63	64	65		
66			67						68					
69			70						71					

FAIRY TALES

ACROSS

1. "The Three Little _____" (29-Down tale)
5. Classic Ford car model: Hyph.
10. Norway's capital
14. Operatic solo
15. "_____ in the court!"
16. Chew like a rat
17. 29-Down character who lost her glass slipper at the ball
19. _____-Red (29-Down character)
20. Suffix with 33-Down
21. "Don't move, doggy!"
22. What Jack's beanstalk did
24. Moo _____ pork (Chinese restaurant dish)
25. Pea container
26. What Hansel was
27. Shake, as a tail
30. Prefix meaning "one"
31. Clearasil may clear it up
32. "Ben-_____" (1959 film that won 11 Oscars)
33. Spaces, as between teeth
36. Storage place for tools
38. Best Picture of 1958
39. "Would _____ to you?": 2 wds.
40. Made less severe
42. Bit of news
43. High cards
44. Cheeselike health food
45. Disease-producing microorganism
46. Say "yes" without speaking
47. Part of a procedure
49. "Judging Amy" network
51. Faucet
52. Word after lily or mouse
53. Slide down a slope
54. Atlas feature
57. Persia, today
59. It rings at the end of class
60. Metal-bearing rock
61. Dummy
63. 29-Down character who wandered into the home of three bears
66. Chamber into which Gretel pushed the witch
67. Whale's home
68. Cincinnati's locale
69. See 5-Down
70. Bitten by a bee
71. _____ Christian Andersen (Danish author of fairy tales)

DOWN

1. Walks back and forth nervously
2. St. Patrick's Day marchers
3. Knife advertised on TV
4. Unhappy
5. Winner of a race against a 69-Across in a 31-Down fable
6. See 23-Down
7. In an inactive way
8. Christianity or Buddhism: Abbr.
9. Fire-breathing fairy tale beast
10. Mean monster of fairy tales
11. 29-Down character who befriended dwarfs: 2 wds.
12. _____ Vegas
13. Have outstanding debts
18. "X-Games" cable station
23. With 6-Down, what some sandwiches are made on
26. Letters after A
28. Carpenter's boring tool
29. Brothers _____ (German brothers Jakob and Wilhelm who collected fairy tales)
30. Avails oneself of
31. Greek author of fables
33. Creature that chased Jack down the beanstalk
34. Big producer of aluminum
35. He rid Hamelin of rats by playing his flute: 2 wds.
37. Despised
38. Jobs for jazz bands
41. "The Ugly _____" (71-Across tale)
47. Health club
48. Ballroom dances

1	2	3	4		5	6	7	8	9		10	11	12	13
14					15						16			
17				18							19			
20					21				22	23				
24					25			26				27	28	29
			30				31					32		
33	34	35			36	37					38			
39					40				41		42			
43						44					45			
46				47	48				49	50				
51				52				53				54	55	56
		57	58				59					60		
61	62				63	64					65			
66					67						68			
69					70						71			

THANKSGIVING

ACROSS

1. Big meal, like the first Thanksgiving dinner
6. Person who frosts a cake
10. Stick a fork into
14. New _____ (capital of India)
15. Treat for the dog
16. Pepsi or Coke
17. 34-Across's middle name
18. With 23-Across, the Pilgrims' agreement to establish a government
20. Low-_____ (indistinct, like computer graphics)
22. _____ cards (fortunetelling tool)
23. See 18-Across
27. Thanksgiving's season
31. "Not a Pretty Girl" singer DiFranco
32. Cheerleader's shout
33. _____ Tin Tin (dog in a 1950's TV series)
34. "The Raven" poet
35. Olympic figure skater Lipinski
37. Area of the United States in which the Pilgrims settled: 2 wds.
40. Pacino and Gore
42. Squeak-stopping stuff
43. Have some 44-Across, for example
44. Thanksgiving dessert: 2 wds.
48. Overflow point of a cup
51. Santa _____, California
52. Suffix with serpent, hero or opal
53. _____ Lanka (country in the Indian Ocean)
55. Garden of Eden resident
56. Confused states: Hyph.
58. The Pilgrims were giving thanks for this at the first Thanksgiving
60. Aware of, in slang: 2 wds.
63. Slide down a slope
64. What students and employees enjoy during Thanksgiving
68. Sci-fi novelist Asimov
72. Jacob's twin in the Bible
73. _____-Rooter (drain-cleaning company)
74. "_____ worry!" ("Never fear!"): 2 wds.
75. Like Shaquille O'Neal
76. Baseball Hall-of-Famer Slaughter
77. It's poured on the Thanksgiving turkey

DOWN

1. Govt. agency concerned with the safety of consumed items
2. "Electric" fish
3. "Can't we _____ just get along?"
4. Like a good knife
5. What a tone-deaf person has: 2 wds.
6. _____-compatible computer
7. Winter outerwear
8. New Age music superstar
9. Song chorus
10. "Party of Five" actor Wolf
11. Stranded motorist's need
12. Ginger _____
13. Soap unit
19. Pass time lazily
21. Read over quickly
23. Garfield is one
24. _____ scale of 1 to 10: 2 wds.
25. Film studio of "Pulp Fiction" and "Trainspotting"
26. Shania Twain's "You're Still _____:" 2 wds.
28. In an embarrassing situation: 3 wds.
29. It's between Sun. and Tue.
30. "_____ & Stacey" (short-lived sitcom)
33. Hot dog topping
36. Swiss mountain
38. Reddi-_____ (brand of dessert topping)
39. Mad scientist's workshop

41. "Never mind": 2 wds.
44. "Mork and Mindy" co-star Dawber
45. Prefix meaning "one"
46. Give an emotional lift to
47. Significant stretches of time
49. Hookups in the E.R.
50. Encountered
54. Ticking off
57. Moving-van rental company: Hyph.
59. Glare blocker attached to a cap
61. "Tiny _____ Adventures" (animated series)
62. "I think you're _____ something!"
64. Doc for a 23-Down
65. Gentle _____ lamb: 2 wds.
66. Ripken of baseball
67. Urgent call for help
69. "One Day _____ Time": 2 wds.
70. Truck designed for on- and off-road: Abbr.
71. Shy

JAPAN

ACROSS

1. Japanese prime minister Hideki who was an Axis general during 9-Down
5. Tae _____ do (aggressive form of karate)
9. "_____ it something I said?"
12. Regions
14. Fashion designer Geoffrey
15. _____ Kosh B'Gosh (brand of kids' clothing)
16. Site of a surprise attack by Japan on a U.S. naval base on December 7, 1941: 2 wds.
18. 17th Greek letter
19. Relation of Japan's Akihito to Hirohito
20. Extremely long time
21. Set to a slow speed, as a fan: 2 wds.
23. Japanese island captured by the U.S. near the end of 9-Down: 2 wds.
27. Emotion-filled poems
28. Japanese sash that wraps around a kimono
30. Supervised
32. How some foods are fried: 2 wds.
34. Tokyo Bay seaport that was the site of a destructive earthquake in 1923
37. "There's Something About Mary" co-star Stiller
38. Letters after D
41. Direction from Tokyo to Osaka: Abbr.
42. Cheerleader's yell
43. U.S. battleship aboard which Japan surrendered to the Allies
46. "You _____ mouthful!": 2 wds.
48. Belief among the Japanese that natural objects and phenomena possess souls
50. Flaky dessert
51. Japan's continent
53. Title of Japanese ruler Akihito
56. "Ready, _____!" (race-starting words): 2 wds.
58. Angry
59. Soap unit
62. Isaac Newton's title
63. Japanese seaport at which the treaty ending the Sino-Japanese War was signed in 1895
68. _____ out a living (live paycheck to paycheck)
69. Plant of the water lily family eaten as a vegetable in Japan
70. Artifact from the past
71. It can be stubbed
72. Had unpaid bills
73. Walking aid

DOWN

1. Phone bugs
2. Black-and-white cookie
3. "Star Trek: The Next Generation" captain _____-Luc Picard
4. Boat paddle
5. Prefix with plop or plunk
6. The third "W" of "WWW"
7. "Should I take that as _____?": 2 wds.
8. Ancient Roman 53-Across
9. 1939–45 conflict in which Japan was one of the Axis powers: 3 wds.
10. "There was an old woman who lived in _____ . . .": 2 wds.
11. Movies, musicals and plays
13. Killed, as a dragon
14. Stringed instrument of bluegrass music
17. "Woo-_____!"
22. Biblical boat builder
23. Half of VI
24. Poison _____ (itch-inducing plant)
25. Cat's comment
26. Boats similar to 22-Down's
28. R.E.M.'s "The _____ Love": 2 wds.
29. Japanese miniature that's grown in a pot and trained to produce a desired shape: 2 wds.
31. Female pigs

32. _____-compatible computer
33. 5th-century pope known as "the Great": 2 wds.
35. "_____ in Japan" (stamp on some products)
36. "I caught you!"
39. Display intense anger
40. _____ Reaper

44. Unforeseen obstacle
45. AOL or Earthlink, for example: Abbr.
47. Month in which the treaty of 63-Across was signed: Abbr.
49. Short office notes
51. Something of value
52. Japanese watch-producing company
54. Participated in a marathon

55. Skunk's defense
57. Capital of Norway
59. Dracula portrayer Lugosi
60. Similar (to)
61. Japanese food staple
64. "_____ are you doing?"
65. Suffix with Tokyo
66. What a pig wallows in
67. "Wait just a _____!"

1	2	3	4			5	6	7	8		9	10	11
12				13		14					15		
16				17							18		
19					20					21	22		
			23				24	25	26		27		
	28	29				30				31			
32				33			34					35	36
37				38	39	40		41				42	
43			44				45			46	47		
		48						49			50		
51	52				53				54	55			
56				57				58				59	60	61
62				63	64	65	66				67		
68				69						70			
71				72						73			

VOLCANOES

ACROSS

1. Site of Olympus Mons, the highest volcano in the solar system
5. Taxis
9. Gush forth, like 61-Across
13. Opera solo
14. Upper heart chambers
16. Possess
17. It's opened on Christmas
18. Martinique volcano that erupted in 1902, destroying the city of St. Pierre: 2 wds.
20. Encountered
21. "Who _____ to say?": 2 wds.
22. Falcons' and Eagles' org.
23. Thomas _____ Edison
25. Linear zone of seismic and volcanic activity that coincides with the Pacific Plate: 3 wds.
30. Kind of committee: 2 wds.
32. Parking place
33. Hair-hardening goop
34. Improvises: Hyph.
36. Chaney of old horror flicks
37. Prefix with trust or toxin
38. "The Jungle Book" bear
39. Alley-_____
40. Regions
41. Regrets bitterly
42. "Earthquake" star Gardner
43. "Finished!": 2 wds.
44. "Don't get _____ ideas"
45. Strike _____ conversation: 2 wds.
46. "The joke's _____!": 2 wds.
47. Washington volcano that had seven major eruptions during 1980: Abbr., 3 wds.
50. Abbr. on an invitation
53. _____-pah-pah (tuba's sound)
54. Zodiac sign
55. "The Crying Game" star Stephen
56. Pertaining to the internal heat of the earth
60. Enter: 2 wds.
61. Molten rock that's expelled from a volcano
62. Nephew's sister
63. Clearasil target
64. Uttered by the mouth
65. Table scraps
66. "The _____ the limit!"

DOWN

1. Molten material beneath the earth's crust from which 27-Down is formed
2. The Little Mermaid's name
3. Elongated undersea chasms in which 1-Down wells up: 2 wds.
4. Occupied a chair
5. Chevy muscle cars
6. Kind of bomb
7. Member of Boston's hockey team
8. Sermon subject
9. Place for books
10. Sidekick
11. Garden of Eden resident
12. Tiny
15. When all a clock's hands are straight up: 2 wds.
19. Sound of something fizzling out
24. "Farewell, amigo!"
26. Unappetizing food
27. Solid matter produced under intense heat, as by solidification of 1-Down: 2 wds.
28. Process a hide again
29. "ER" actress Christine _____
31. Alternative to Cinemax or Showtime
34. James _____ Garfield
35. Intimidate
36. Mauna _____ (world's largest active volcano)
37. Intense eagerness
39. Ellipse
40. "Judging _____" (CBS show)
42. Tarzan and Greystoke: Hyph.
43. Arched shoe parts

THE ELECTORAL PROCESS

ACROSS

1. _____ a ballot (enter votes)
5. "... even _____ speak": 2 wds.
9. Network that airs "Frasier" and "Friends"
12. "... to fetch _____ of water": 2 wds.
14. _____ out (go nuts)
15. Suffix with schnozz
16. Number 2 person on a political ticket: 2 wds.
18. You can clean the floor with it
19. "Winnie the _____"
20. Game show hosts, for short
21. "Sands of _____ Jima" (classic World War II film)
22. Wrestler Hulk and actor Paul
25. "_____ humbug!"
26. "What's _____ for me?": 2 wds.
27. Signs of the future
28. One of the people to choose from on Election Day
30. Fourth planet from the sun
31. "The Fresh Prince of _____-Air"
32. Newspaper notice, for short
33. Make a mistake
34. Electoral _____ (body that elects the President and Vice President)
36. Huge computer corp.
39. Village People hit with hand motions
41. Takes too much, for short
42. Elizabeth _____ (28-Across in the 2000 Presidential race)
43. Republicans' opponents
46. Lists of options
47. _____ Keyes (28-Across in the 2000 Presidential race)
48. Workers in the E.R. and O.R.
49. Minor memory failures
50. Homo sapiens
51. "Where do _____ from here?": 2 wds.
52. "Runaway Bride" star Richard
53. Prefix with term, night or west
54. Trying to win the support of voters
59. Dallas-to-Nashville direction: Abbr.
60. Letter sent over the Internet
61. "Dr. Dolittle" star Murphy
62. "Dawson's Creek" star James Van _____ Beek
63. What a student crams for
64. Shoe bottom

DOWN

1. Bumper sticker site
2. Storekeeper on "The Simpsons"
3. _____ Francisco, Calif.
4. Lightweight metal cake containers: 2 wds.
5. Bracelet site
6. Sailor
7. They bark when strangers enter the house
8. _____ out a living (barely scrapes by)
9. Results from political conventions
10. Really mess up: 2 wds
11. "Breakfast at Tiffany's" author Truman _____
13. Detroit football team
14. Letters between E and I
17. Negative votes
22. The "H" of "HBO"
23. "The Mod Squad" co-star Epps
24. Division of a state into imbalanced election districts
25. Voters make their choices on them
26. Ugandan tyrant _____ Amin
28. Animation sheet
29. "How can _____ sure?": 2 wds
31. Monopoly, chess or Risk: 2 wds.
34. 300, in Roman numerals
35. Actors Asner and Harris
37. Color of 46-Down's hair
38. Disorder
40. It's between Sun. and Tue.
42. Relies (on)

43. Stopped up, as a river
44. One of Seinfeld's friends
45. Fragrances
46. Homer Simpson's wife
49. Hawaiian necklace
51. Rapper-turned-actor
52. _____ pal (girlfriend)
55. Nectarine center
56. Wedding promise: 2 wds.
57. Nothing
58. "_____ whiz!"

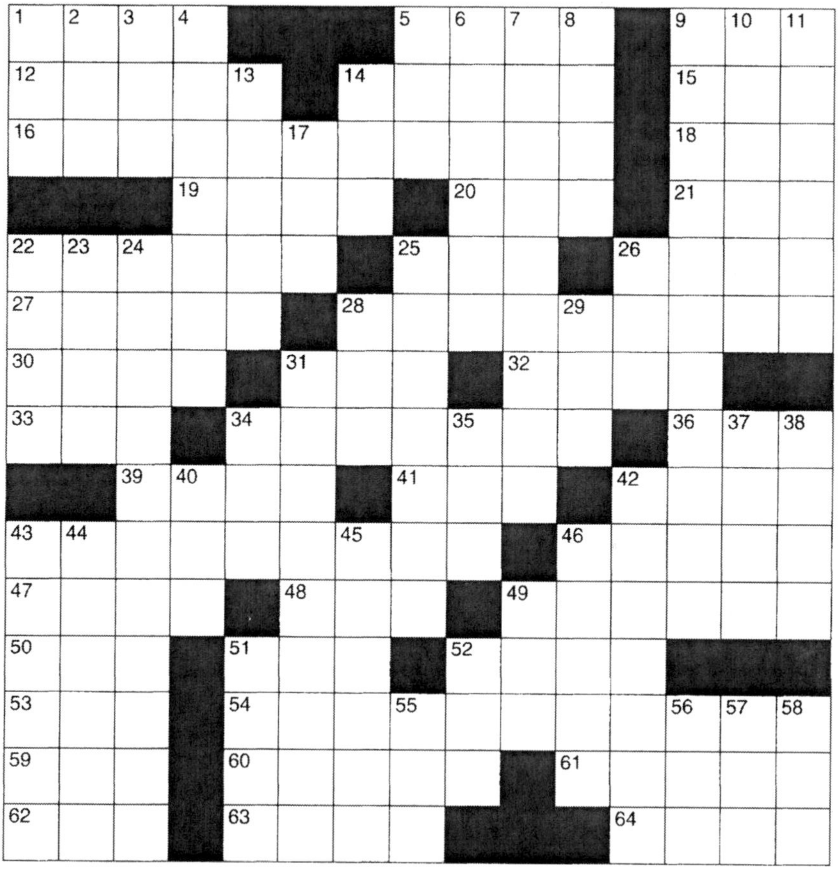

ROCKS AND MINERALS

ACROSS

1. Translucent, milky white gems
6. In need of a backrub
11. Angry
14. "Dawson's Creek" actress Holmes
15. Vines that crawl up the sides of buildings
16. Female sheep
17. Icicle-shaped deposits on the roof of a cave
19. Phone bug
20. Liquefied by heat, as volcanic rock
21. Autumn lawn tool
22. Brothers and sisters, for short
26. Vegetable in a pod
27. Baby shower attendees, usually
28. Process of sorting accident victims to determine medical priority
30. Precious gem that is the hardest substance known to man
32. Major artery out of the heart
33. "Mystery Men" actor Ben
35. Blasting stuff
36. Green gem that is a rare variety of beryl
38. Paid athlete
41. Forms of sodium chloride in cubic crystals
43. "Hamlet" star Hawke

45. Remnants of the distant past, as animal outlines etched into rocks
47. Don't take "no" for an answer
48. Dusty storage room
49. "Cool!"
51. Bounced-back sound
52. Dovish murmurs
53. Gems formed within the shells of mollusks
56. Charged particle
57. Like rocks that are formed from mineral or organic matter deposited by water, air or ice
62. Ginger ____
63. Get out of bed
64. Possessed
65. "____ Misérables" (Victor Hugo classic)
66. Toned down, as some trumpets
67. Lines of alternating color, as those present in onyx

DOWN

1. Gives the go-ahead
2. Butter serving
3. ____ loss for words: 2 wds.
4. Rapper ____ Kim
5. Line formed by sewing together pieces of cloth
6. Name given to a movie or song
7. 1996 Madonna musical
8. "Nick at ____"

(Nickelodeon lineup)
9. "Now I've ____ everything!"
10. Letter on Superman's chest
11. Exhibiting structural change, as some rocks
12. Stop sleeping
13. Rely (on)
18. Handle hardship
21. Italy's capital
22. Age, height or weight
23. Element found in raw form in metal-bearing mineral or rock
24. Precious or semiprecious gems associated with particular months
25. Occupied a chair
27. ____ books (major bookstore chain)
29. Language spoken in Ireland
30. "Buenos ____!" (Spanish for "Good day!")
31. Sick
33. Mounts in a frame, as a gem
34. Three, in 21-Down
37. $1,000,000, slangily
39. Allergic skin reaction
40. "I think you're ____ something!"
42. Phrase on a garage sale tag: 2 wds.

44. Communist chairman Mao _____ -tung

45. _____ hair (beard and mustache)

46. "Lawrence of Arabia" star Peter

47. Keep the engine running without driving

49. Pay increase

50. Equipped with weapons

53. South American country with a wealth of mineral resources

54. Prepare for publication

55. Stuck-up person

57. "Summer of _____" (1999 Spike Lee movie)

58. US Airways competitor

59. _____ Arbor, Michigan

60. Color of rubies and garnets

61. Units of three feet; Abbr.

1	2	3	4	5		6	7	8	9	10		11	12	13
14						15						16		
17				18								19		
				20							21			
22	23	24	25		26					27				
28				29			30	31						
32					33	34								
35			36	37							38	39	40	
		41	42						43	44				
45	46					47								
48					49	50			51					
52				53	54			55						
56			57						58	59	60	61		
62			63				64							
65			66				67							

CIVIL RIGHTS AND FREEDOMS

ACROSS

1. Separation of church and ___ (topic of the First Amendment)
6. What a wound might do
11. Avenues: Abbr.
14. Gave a hoot
15. Pound division
16. Before, to poets
17. Bringing together of formerly separated races
19. Refuse to agree to
20. Got close to
21. French holy woman: Abbr.
23. One who oversees the employees: Abbr.
26. N.F.L. six-pointers
27. Drinking vessel in a Chinese restaurant
30. Having only a single section, as a short play: Hyph.
33. Illinois city next to Champaign
34. This was started in Montgomery when Rosa Parks was arrested for refusing to give up her seat: 2 wds.
38. National Association ___ the Advancement of Colored People (N.A.A.C.P.)
39. Psychic power
40. Leann Rimes' "How ___ Live?": 2 wds.
41. Alternative to Delta or US Airways
43. Hockey Hall-of-Famer Bobby
45. State ordinance discriminating against blacks: 3 wds.
49. Greet with a hand motion: 2 wds.
52. "The Mighty Ducks" star Estevez
53. National Urban ___ (group working against racial segregation and discrimination)
54. Steambath site
56. ___-mo replay
57. Heavy weight
58. ___ off (repelled)
61. Moo goo ___ pan (Chinese dish)
63. Martin Luther King Jr.'s famous phrase: 4 wds.
68. "A long time ___ in a galaxy . . ."
69. Clowns wear big red ones
70. Hospital worker in white
71. Japanese coin
72. First, reverse and neutral
73. One more time

DOWN

1. The ___-Fi Channel
2. Beige
3. Paintings, sculptures, etc.
4. "Dawson's Creek" watcher, usually
5. A razor has a sharp one
6. Brown v. ___ of Education (1954 case in which segregation in public schools was ruled unconstitutional)
7. Stringed instruments played by minstrels
8. Barenaked Ladies song from "Gordon"
9. ___-friendly (not harmful to the environment)
10. More tightly packed together
11. ___ Convention (1848 women's rights conference organized by Elizabeth Cady Stanton and Lucretia Mott): 2 wds.
12. Prefix meaning "three"
13. The 19th Amendment guaranteed that voting rights were not restricted based on this
18. Dilapidated
22. Soda can opener
23. Disorderly crowd
24. African antelope also known as a wildebeest
25. Tract of land set apart for the use of an Indian tribe
27. Egyptian boy-king
28. Game with "Reverse" cards
29. Good score for a golfer
31. Tummy muscles
32. Speeding ticket issuer
35. 401, in Roman numerals
36. ___-pah-pah (tuba's sound)
37. ___-tac-toe
41. "Saving Private Ryan" star Hanks
42. Global conflict of 1914–18: Abbr.
43. Bird that hoots at night

44. "Mask of Death" actress _____ Dawn Chong

45. Quarterback Montana

46. _____ book (be literate): 2 wds.

47. Feel sick

48. Try to win the affection of

50. Self-importance

51. Correcting a piano

54. One who makes regular bank deposits

55. Freedom of the _____ (topic of the First Amendment)

58. "That _____ close one!": 2 wds.

59. "The Simpsons" schoolteacher Krabappel

60. Caffeine or nicotine, for example

61. _____ rights movement (organized effort to stop discrimination based on sexual orientation)

62. What tree rings indicate

64. Weed-whacking tool

65. Proposed 27th amendment that would prohibit sexual discrimination: Abbr.

66. "Just _____ thought!": 2 wds.

67. ". . . all _____ are created equal!"

1	2	3	4	5		6	7	8	9	10		11	12	13
14						15						16		
17				18								19		
			20							21	22			
23	24	25			26				27				28	29
30			31	32					33					
34					35	36	37					38		
		39				40				41	42			
43	44				45			46					47	48
49			50	51					52					
53							54	55				56		
		57				58				59	60			
61	62			63	64							65	66	67
68				69						70				
71				72						73				

TALES OF TERROR

ACROSS

1. See 37-Down
5. Actor Jean-_____ Van Damme
11. Lifesaving medical technique, for short
14. 43,560 square feet
15. Genre of 38-Across and 67-Across
16. "_____ Haw" (long-running variety show)
17. Master of 15-Across: 2 wds.
19. Stimpy's cartoon sidekick
20. Caffeinated beverage
21. End of some E-mail addresses
22. It may be stuffed with pimento
24. Son of Herman and Lily Munster
26. Tale of heroism
30. "That makes sense": 2 wds.
31. Letters between B and F
33. It's used to draw water from a well
35. "The _____ Half" (novel by 17-Across)
38. Novel by 17-Across: 2 wds.
42. "Evil Woman" rock band, for short
43. Moo _____ pork
44. "Home Improvement" star Allen
45. MTV hostess Peeples
46. "The Legend of Sleepy Hollow" author Irving
49. Fishes with electric organs
50. More like a 17-Across novel
51. Young lady in a square dance
53. Wile E. Coyote's preferred brand
55. "Skeleton _____" (book by 17-Across)
57. "Saturday Night Fever" music
61. Actors Pitt and Renfro
63. "Tales From the Crypt" broadcaster
65. Preschooler
66. Lobed body part
67. 1982 ghost flick with two sequels
72. "Don't get _____ ideas"
73. TV's "Mistress of the Dark"
74. Opening poker contribution
75. Hi-_____ graphics
76. Does preflight airplane maintenance in winter
77. Rip

DOWN

1. Moisten in the oven, as a turkey
2. Played a part
3. Sandwich need
4. Opposite of "nope"
5. "Believe" singer
6. Yearns (for)
7. Noah's boat
8. Geller with supposed mental powers
9. "Nash Bridges" star Johnson
10. Therefore
11. Novel by 17-Across
12. Pet _____ (continual annoyance)
13. "One True Thing" actress Zellweger
18. Used a long-handled garden tool
23. Property claim
25. "Eeew!"
27. President Lincoln, familiarly
28. Enthusiasm
29. Sore, as a back
32. _____ group (people sharing a common culture)
34. Basinger of "L.A. Confidential"
35. Morning droplets on grass
36. Pie _____ mode: 2 wds.
37. With 1-Across, Ira Levin novel made into a 1968 film
39. More enormous
40. Nothing
41. It's pumped into a car
43. Title for Andrew Lloyd Webber or Ian McKellen
47. Pay attention to
48. Italian for "three"
49. Cotton gin inventor Whitney

52. Sick as _____: 2 wds.
53. "Fuzzy Wuzzy was _____ . . .": 2 wds.
54. "The Legend of Sleepy Hollow" character Ichabod _____
56. In which place
58. "Goosebumps" series author R. L. _____
59. _____ Rica (Central American country)
60. Playful aquatic mammal
62. Floored it
64. Bikini tops
68. "Bravo!", at a bullfight
69. 56, in Roman numerals
70. _____-tac-toe
71. Scarf down

1	2	3	4	■	5	6	7	8	9	10	■	11	12	13
14				■	15						■	16		
17				18							■	19		
20			■	21			■			22	23			
24			25			■	26	27	28	29	■	30		
■			31		32	■	33			34			■	
35	36	37		■	38	39							40	41
42			■	43			■	44			■	45		
46			47			48			■	49				
■		50				■		51	52		■			
53	54			■	55		56	■	57		58	59	60	
61			62	■			63	64		■	65			
66			■	67	68	69	70			71				
72			■	73				■		74				
75			■	76						77				

SUMMER VACATION

ACROSS

1. Have fun outside on a summer day
5. Homes away from home during the summer
10. Battery liquid
14. Singer/politician Sonny
15. Regions
16. "WKRP in Cincinnati" actress Anderson
17. What you can do on summer vacation nights: 3 wds.
19. Mouth off to
20. Frequently
21. Substance violinists apply to their bows
22. Oboe's relative
25. Actress West of old films
27. Communist leader Mao _____-tung
28. "It's no _____!"
29. Summer vacation getaway
31. Hog's home
32. _____ Beach, Florida (summer 29-Across)
35. Waiters carry them
37. Fun place to visit during summer vacation: 2 wds.
42. Blinding light
43. Swords used in an Olympic event
45. Summer _____ (student's money source)
48. Turns away, as the eyes
51. "Don't _____ on it!"
52. When the plane is expected to land, approximately: Abbr.
53. Homer's neighbor on "The Simpsons"
54. Wheel covers
57. See 13-Down
59. Hazard
60. Tiny bit
61. Holiday date during summer vacation: 2 wds.
66. Vehicle stored away during the summer
67. Love, Italian-style
68. Tiresome person
69. Not his
70. Didn't 71-Across
71. Enjoy the pool during summer vacation

DOWN

1. "Sesame Street" network
2. Parking _____
3. Santa _____, California
4. Toys that go up and down
5. Hostage holder
6. "Journey to the Center of the Earth" actress Dahl
7. Unkind
8. "Wheel of Fortune" host Sajak
9. Direction from Dallas to Houston: Abbr.
10. Furthermore
11. Beach-lovers' summer vacation spots
12. Not take "no" for an answer
13. With 57-Across, themed vacation spot in Orlando, Florida
18. "The X-Files" sighting
21. Key in again
22. Beach _____ (lover of 11-Down)
23. Cambodia's continent
24. Sewing line
25. Daybreak, for short
26. "I smell _____!": 2 wds.
30. Have control of the wheel
33. Coffee container
34. Summer vacation destination, often
36. Tree drippings
38. Overhanging part of a roof
39. Talking horse of TV: 2 wds.
40. Country singer McEntire
41. "_____ up the good work!"
44. Avenues: Abbr.
45. Like most Tel Aviv residents
46. "Lawrence of Arabia" star Peter
47. Trade
49. "_____ here!" ("Poltergeist" catchphrase)
50. Enjoyed the waves in summer
55. High school class, for short
56. Not diamonds, hearts or spades
58. Schoolboys

59. Walk heavily
61. Jay Leno's prominent facial feature
62. "The Avengers" co-star Thurman
63. Use the oars
64. Prefix meaning "three"
65. Sewing line

Do you want
even MORE?

Solve our daily, weekend and Sunday Magazine puzzles online,
FREE OF CHARGE for one month.

Premium Crosswords offers access to over 2,000 New York Times crossword puzzles.*
This is an exclusive one-time offer.**

Plus you can:

❏ Play today's New York Times puzzle.

❏ Download puzzles to play online or print to solve offline.

❏ Play five years of daily & weekend puzzles (with solutions).

❏ Play both puzzles from the Sunday Magazine.

❏ Solve acrostics, Web-only puzzles and much more.

*Premium Crosswords subscription is $19.95 annually (as of 8/01). NYTimes.com reserves the right to change
these prices at anytime without notice. **You will be required to supply credit card information when registering for
the free 30-day period. After the free 30-day period you will be prompted to enroll as an annual Premium Crossword
subscriber. If you elect not to subscribe you will incur no charges. If you elect to become an annual subscriber, the
credit card supplied during registration will be charged. Your annual subscription will be automatically renewed
every year unless you cancel. We hope you enjoy your free 30 days of Premium Crosswords.

NYTimes.com/freepuzzles

THE 50 STATES

```
L A N D ■ N E V A D A ■ B O B
E W E R ■ A L I S O N ■ R T E
O L D D O M I N I O N ■ I T T
■ R U E ■ Y A W ■ ■ S A T
S A F E S ■ ■ O N E T W O
L I L ■ T U L I P P O P L A R
I R I S ■ S H O E ■ I C E ■
T E C H ■ S A W E R ■ O C T A
■ K A T ■ S A V E ■ T O U T
A M E R I C A N E L M ■ N B A
M E R I N O ■ ■ O C E A N
E X T ■ A G O ■ A N A ■
N I A ■ G R A N D C A N Y O N
D C I ■ E S T E E M ■ A E R O
S O L ■ N E E D L E ■ L A S T
```

NATIVE AMERICAN HISTORY

```
I N C A ■ M U R A L S ■ T U T
F A I R ■ O R E G O N ■ O P E
S I T T I N G B U L L ■ T O T
O L E ■ T R E A T ■ R E N O
■ G O O ■ ■ S H A M A N
L O P E ■ E W E ■ C A M P ■
A R O M A ■ A T L A S ■ O P S
S E C ■ B I G H O R N ■ L E T
T O A ■ O C E A N ■ T H E R E
■ H A V E ■ N E T ■ I S U P
A D O B E S ■ ■ E N D ■
N U N S ■ T E M P O ■ I N K
D E T ■ W O U N D E D K N E E
E T A ■ E N T I C E ■ E R I E
S O S ■ S A U D I S ■ Y E L P
```

FAMOUS ARTISTS AND WORKS

```
D A L I ■ D A N C E ■ K I M
I D O L ■ S A L O O N ■ E R A
P A U L C E Z A N N E ■ I A N
■ O V E R ■ ■ O T T O
T A M A L E ■ M C E S C H E R
I M A G E R Y ■ H E A T H
M I R E ■ O P A L S ■ A R C
I N C ■ N O U R I S H ■ R E O
D O C ■ E M B E R ■ V I N E
■ H O R N E ■ S T A I N E D
G R A F F I T I ■ A D A G E S
R I G A ■ ■ N O T A ■
O V A ■ C L A U D E M O N E T
V A L ■ D E N S E R ■ I R O N
E L L ■ S I D E S ■ L A S T
```

AUTHORS AND LITERATURE

```
J A N E ■ E Y R E ■ E T H A N
A W O L ■ D E A R ■ D I E G O
M A R K T W A I N ■ D A M E S
E R S ■ H A R L E Y ■ R I S E
S E E ■ O R B ■ S A G A N
■ J U D O ■ T W O ■ G E L
A W H O ■ S O B ■ S U B W A Y
B E A K S ■ K O S ■ P E A R L
O R W E L L ■ O W E ■ T Y P E
Y E T ■ A I M ■ E B B S ■
■ H I T S A ■ E W E ■ G U M
P O O R ■ A R E T H A ■ R N A
O P R A H ■ S T E I N B E C K
D A N T E ■ H O S T ■ B A L E
S L E E P ■ A N T E ■ S T E R
```

ELECTRICITY AND MAGNETISM

A	T	O	M		R	E	C	I	P	E		A	P	P
N	A	M	E		E	D	I	S	O	N		T	O	A
T	R	A	N	S	I	S	T	O	R	S		T	L	C
S	T	R	U	T	S		E	N	E		B	R	E	T
		S	E	E	M	S		C	R	A	S	S		
S	I	C		A	R	C		S	P	E	C			
A	R	O	C	K		I	N	S	U	L	A	T	O	R
M	O	N	A		P	I	E	I	N		T	I	N	A
I	N	D	U	C	T	I	O	N		S	H	O	C	K
		U	S	D	A		U	M	A		N	E	E	
F	A	C	E	S		U	S	U	R	P				
O	P	T	S		F	U	N		R	A	I	S	E	S
R	E	O		B	E	N	F	R	A	N	K	L	I	N
C	A	R		O	R	D	E	A	L		E	U	R	O
E	R	S		A	N	O	D	E	S		D	R	E	W

WOMEN'S HISTORY

T	A	R	A		S	A	S	H		A	L	M	A
O	R	A	L		A	L	I	K	E		L	E	A	F
M	A	R	I	E	C	U	R	I	E		M	A	Y	A
S	T	E	E	L	E	R		E	L	E	A	N	O	R
			N	O	D		A	R	S	O	N			
C	L	A	S	P		I	R	S		N	A	D	I	A
E	L	I		E	L	S	A		A	S	C	E	N	D
D	A	D	S		E	M	I	L	Y		S	P	U	D
A	M	E	L	I	A		S	I	N	G		T	S	E
R	A	D	I	O		S	I	B		O	O	H	E	D
		T	W	A	I	N		I	N	N				
E	A	R	H	A	R	T		A	N	N	E	T	T	E
A	L	O	E		I	C	E	S	K	A	T	E	R	S
S	T	A	R		S	O	L	E	S		W	A	I	T
T	O	R	Y		E	M	M	A			O	L	G	A

20TH CENTURY INNOVATIONS

M	O	D	E	M		A	N	E	Y	E		C	P	R
A	N	A	X	E		C	A	R	D	S		A	L	I
C	O	M	P	A	C	T	D	I	S	C		L	A	B
			O	N	L	O	A	N			P	C	S	
T	E	L		S	I	N		A	S	T	U	T	E	
E	L	I	A		P	E	N	I	C	I	L	L	I	N
A	L	E	R	O	S		O	T	H	E		A	C	E
		D	E	R		P	T	A		G	O	T		
U	N	E		G	E	A	R		S	E	C	O	N	D
N	U	T	R	A	S	W	E	E	T		T	R	O	N
O	C	E	A	N	S		R	E	D		S	P	A	
	L	C	D		P	H	O	N	E	S				
S	E	T		S	P	E	E	D	O	M	E	T	E	R
S	A	O		A	S	O	R	E		O	M	E	G	A
E	R	R		L	I	N	E	S		N	I	X	O	N

MYTHOLOGY

L	A	G		O	L	D	M	A	N		B	O	A	T
O	N	O		P	A	R	A	D	E		A	C	R	E
U	N	D	E	R	W	O	R	L	D		P	E	K	E
		D	A	Y		L	I	I		E	T	A		
A	R	E	S			L	A	B	Y	R	I	N	T	H
O	B	S	E	S	S			E	N	S	U	R	E	
L	I	S		G	L	O	B	A	L		T	S	A	R
		M	T	O	L	Y	M	P	U	S				
L	O	C	O		G	A	S	P	E	R		B	A	A
E	U	R	O	P	A			D	I	S	A	R	M	
T	R	O	J	A	N	W	A	R		A	C	T	S	
	S	U	N		H	U	E		T	L	C			
W	A	S	I		K	I	N	G	A	R	T	H	U	R
A	L	E	C		I	N	T	I	M	E		U	R	N
D	A	D	E		N	E	S	S	I	E		S	E	A

THE HUMAN BODY

PEOPLE OF THE MILLENNIUM

THE MIDDLE AGES

INSECTS

MUSIC

```
P O P   T E E T H   A S C A P
I S A   A N D R E   C E L L O
A C C O R D I O N   S C A L E
N A T O   S T I N G     S I T
O R S O N     S E R I E S
      A W E   R O L L I N G
A D D   T O R I   A L I C I A
L E I S   O R G A N   S A L T
P L A C I D   O V E R   L E E
S I N A T R A   E R A
  A B S O R B     P A N T S
E A R   W I R E D   S O U L
L L O Y D   S A X O P H O N E
L A S E R   E V I T A   S E E
S I S S Y   N O T E S   E S P
```

TALES OF MYSTERY AND SUSPENSE

```
D I A L M   H A R D Y   T K O
E S S E S   A L A N A   H I D
J O H N G R I S H A M   E L I
A N Y   C R O     I S L E
    L A A   S T A S H
C I G A R   D E T E C T I V E
A R O S E   E L U D E   N I B
R I O T   B E T A S   R I C O
A S S   A R M O R   C O N A N
T H E C L I E N T   A N G R Y
  B U S E D   A B S
C L U E   I L L   I N D
O O M   H A R R Y P O T T E R
R I P   A R B O R   O R S O N
E S S   S T I N E   P I A N O
```

WEATHER

```
H A I L   L O T S A   T D S
O I L O F   A T W A R   E R A
P R E C I P I T A T E   M E L
  A B E   O N O   P A T
O C T   B L T   G U S T E D
F O R   E V E   S T A R R
F L O O D I N G   L E A F S
O O P S   S N O W S   S T O P
F R O S T   P R E S S U R E
  S I E G E   A T E   R C A
  O P E N E D   P T A   E E K
S H H   N I X   E S P
M A E   M E T E O R O L O G Y
O R R   A R E N A   N A B O O
G E E   R A D A R   N I N O
```

BLACK HISTORY MONTH

```
R O S A   S A G S   F A N
O P A L   T R O T   A L I C E
B I L L C O S B Y   M O T H S
S E T   A W O L   A M A Z E S
  I R E N E   C O N G
O S C A R   S T A R   S E A T
P H O N I C   S T U N   R I O
R A N   E R A   E S E   A R M
A R F   D I S C   H A R L E M
H E E D   S H O P   T E D D Y
  R E M I   N O S E D
O P E R A S   T W I N   T O E
G O N E R   D R E D S C O T T
L O C K E   R O L E   U N I T
E R E   E L L A   P I S A
```

U.S. PRESIDENTS

```
HAYES . POLK . JAN
INALL ROUGE . AMI
JIMMYCARTER . MIX
. ELECT . . LENO
. THOSE . HARRISON
TRAITOR . HELM .
EARL . ATSEA . OTT
AIR ABRAHAM . NYE
STY NIECE . URLS
. TODD . DINGOES
GARFIELD . TOHER
ABUT . AIMAT . .
TOM . BILLCLINTON
EVA ICALL . NOWWE
SEN . NEWS . GRANT
```

THE ROARING TWENTIES

```
AGE USA . TUV . CBS
ROD SATCHMO . HIT
MONKEYTRIAL . AGO
SPAN . NOS . VIRGO
. OER . BOOTLEG
BOBBYJONES . WERE
UNI . ERIE . ERAS
BANJO DRY ASTRO
. GUNN . VENI . OAK
ABCS . PRESIDENTS
NURTURE . ASA .
GROAN MCV . SOLO
ENS . PROHIBITION
RUB OCTOBER . LOL
SPY TAE . ENE SKY
```

BIODIVERSITY

```
HOARD SLAP . GOAT
OTTER COMB . RULE
RHINOCEROS . ASIA
NET PONY . ASTER
. HOLE . DENS .
SPROUT . PANTHERS
POINT SLID . OVAL
LACE FOURS PIKE
ICKY ARMY . OPTED
THISTLES KNEADS
. URLS . DEER .
FANCY . TALC . THO
REEK WOODPECKER
ORAL AULD LIONS
GORE LILY . LASSO
```

NATIONAL POETRY MONTH

```
LAST . EGO . EMCEE
ALAS SLOW NEARS
DICKINSON DANES
YES SUED . ISNT
. DIG MAN TEST
ASSET WADSWORTH
PATS DENVER BEA
III JAI ICY URN
ELL ARREST TREK
COLERIDGE YOYOS
ERIN NOG DAY .
. RANG RAIN . PSI
PRIME JOHNKEATS
EASES OLEO BLUE
PEELS ELM . BONE
```

AFRICA

```
S N O W   S N A C K   K O P  
T O D O   W I T H E R   I R E  
S I E R R A L E O N E   L I P  
    L O M E   P Y G M I E S  
V E R D E     S P A   O M N I  
E T A S   C L A Y   S W A T S  
T R I   A H O Y   A T E N    
S E N E G A L   A B I D J A N
  F E U D   B O E R   A P U  
A D O R E   L U K E   T R E K
S A R I   P E G   C H O S E  
C H E E T A H   V A S E    
E L S   B U R K I N A F A S O
N I T   S L E E V E   L I O N
D A S     A R R O W   U R N S
```

LONGITUDE & LATITUDE

```
R E N O   F R O M   O M A N
U R A L   L O D I   A F A C T
N I L E R I V E R   S O U T H
T E A   E N E     S P U R  
      T N T   S U P E R I O R
I R W I N   D I G I N   T A I
D E A N E   I R A N   A R F
E D S   S A C   N Y E   N I L
A S H   B I R D   M A I N E
L E I   G E N O A   B R A G S
S A N D I E G O   S R I  
  G E N T   Y A Y   A B A
T A T A S   D E S M O I N E S
U P O L U   O R E O   L O R I
B E N T   T A R A   E N N A
```

NUTRITION

```
D A I R Y   S A L E   U S E
E D G E I N   T R O N   N O G
F O O D P Y R A M I D   S A G
    D E C O R   S U G A R S
  A V E   M C D   P O T  
S C E N T S   H E W   T U F T
L E G   R U B   C A L O R I E
A T E   I S O   A T O   A B E
V I T A M I N   F E R   T E N
S C A M   E E N   R I D E R S
  R E F   S U E   I D S
G R I N A T   C R A I G  
R E A   C H O L E S T E R O L
A N N   T A K E   P A S T R Y
M O S   S I S I   S T E R N
```

PAGE ONE

```
E A R   H A L T S   C O M I C
E R E   O N E A L   O P E R A
L E A D S T O R Y   P A R E S
S A D N E S S   B Y L I N E
  E A S Y   F O U R   T E D
E R R   R U B R I C  
C O A C H   E N E   G I S T
O L D I E   A N Y   H A Y E S
  E S T A   L I E   T O N T O
    E D I T E D   D E W
P T A   L A Y S   T H A I
L E F T I N   C H O I C E S
U N I O N   N A M E P L A T E
M O R S E   A D O R E   T O N
P R E S S   B O N E S   E N D
```

CHINA

PLACES AND REGIONS

IMMIGRATION

THE CIVIL WAR

ANIMAL LIFE CYCLES

```
L A R V A  .  C H I C  .  .  I S M
A R I E S  .  L M N O  .  A N N A
G E S T A T I O N S  .  S C A T
S S E  .  P U P S  .  M A T U R E
 .  R I B  .  S O F A B E D
E T H A N  .  C A W  .  I R A  .
G R A M  .  A L P E R T  .  T A N
G U T S  .  P U P A E  .  W I N E
S E C  .  S T I L T S  .  E O N S
 .  H A L  .  N E S  .  M A N E T
M O L T I N G  .  .  D A N  .
A R I S T A  .  S C U M  .  S P A
R E N E  .  P H E R O M O N E S
T O G A  .  E A T A  .  A D U L T
S S S  .  .  S T A G  .  L E G T O
```

THE AMERICAN REVOLUTION

```
S T A R  .  S O N S  .  .  T A T
H O S E  .  S A Y N O  .  D I V E
E T H A N A L L E N  .  A C I D
 .  C E N T  .  A R N O L D
F A C T S  .  M A R E  .  N A Y
I T O  .  S E D A N  .  B O D  .
R E M I  .  R E D D  .  A R E N A
S A M S  .  A F I R E  .  A R I D
T R O L L  .  U S E R  .  L O C A
 .  N E O  .  S O W E D  .  G E M
S O S  .  O M E N  .  .  Y E A R S
T R E A T Y  .  A B E T  .
A I N T  .  B U N K E R H I L L
L O S E  .  A N N I E  .  E R I E
E N E  .  D O W N  .  L A T E
```

ARCHAEOLOGY

```
M A P S  .  W H A R F S  .  E B B
A B E T  .  A U R O R A  .  X I I
T U T A N K H A M E N  .  C O S
 .  T O E  .  B E E  .  M A N E
M E R I T  .  .  S L A V I C
E N A C T S  .  A R T I F A C T
S O D  .  O U T D O  .  P I T  .
A S I A  .  P O E T S  .  A I D S
 .  O N U  .  O A S I S  .  O O P
B A C K F I L L  .  R U N N E R
A V A L O N  .  .  S I S S Y
L I R E  .  S A W  .  S H E  .
L A B  .  M A C H U P I C C H U
A T O  .  I N T A K E  .  E R A S
D E N  .  T E S T E D  .  S O M E
```

FAIRY TALES

```
P I G S  .  T B I R D  .  O S L O
A R I A  .  O R D E R  .  G N A W
C I N D E R E L L A  .  R O S E
E S S  .  S T A Y  .  G R E W  .
S H U  .  P O D  .  B O Y  .  W A G
 .  U N I  .  A C N E  .  H U R
G A P S  .  S H E D  .  G I G I
I L I E  .  E A S E D  .  I T E M
A C E S  .  T O F U  .  G E R M
N O D  .  S T E P  .  C B S  .
T A P  .  P A D  .  S K I  .  M A P
 .  I R A N  .  B E L L  .  O R E
D O P E  .  G O L D I L O C K S
O V E N  .  O C E A N  .  O H I O
H A R E  .  S T U N G  .  H A N S
```

THANKSGIVING

JAPAN

VOLCANOES

THE ELECTORAL PROCESS

ROCKS AND MINERALS

```
O P A L S   ■ T E N S E ■ M A D
K A T I E   ■ I V I E S ■ E W E
S T A L A C T I T E S ■ T A P
■ ■ M O L T E N ■ R A K E
S I B S ■ P E A ■ W O M E N
T R I A G E ■ D I A M O N D
A O R T A ■ S T I L L E R ■
T N T ■ E M E R A L D ■ P R O
■ H A L I T E S ■ E T H A N
F O S S I L S ■ I N S I S T
A T T I C ■ R A D ■ E C H O
C O O S ■ P E A R L S
I O N ■ S E D I M E N T A R Y
A L E ■ A R I S E ■ O W N E D
L E S ■ M U T E D ■ B A N D S
```

CIVIL RIGHTS AND FREEDOMS

```
S T A T E ■ B L E E D ■ S T S
C A R E D ■ O U N C E ■ E R E
I N T E G R A T I O N ■ N I X
■ N E A R E D ■ S T E ■
M G R ■ T D S ■ T E A C U P
O N E A C T ■ U R B A N A
B U S B O Y C O T T ■ F O R
■ E S P ■ D O I ■ T W A
O R R ■ J I M C R O W L A W
W A V E T O ■ E M I L I O
L E A G U E ■ S P A ■ S L O
■ T O N ■ W A R D E D
G A I ■ I H A V E A D R E A M
A G O ■ N O S E S ■ N U R S E
Y E N ■ G E A R S ■ A G A I N
```

TALES OF TERROR

```
B A B Y ■ C L A U D E ■ C P R
A C R E ■ H O R R O R ■ H E E
S T E P H E N K I N G ■ R E N
T E A ■ O R G ■ O L I V E
E D D I E ■ S A G A ■ I S E E
■ C D E ■ B U C K E T ■
D A R K ■ T H E S H I N I N G
E L O ■ S H U ■ T I M ■ N I A
W A S H I N G T O N ■ E E L S
■ E E R I E R ■ G A L
A C M E ■ C R E W ■ D I S C O
B R A D S ■ H B O ■ T O T
E A R ■ P O L T E R G E I S T
A N Y ■ E L V I R A ■ A N T E
R E S ■ D E I C E S ■ T E A R
```

SUMMER VACATION

```
P L A Y ■ C A M P S ■ A C I D
B O N O ■ A R E A S ■ L O N I
S T A Y U P L A T E ■ S A S S
■ O F T E N ■ R O S I N
B A S S O O N ■ M A E ■ T S E
U S E ■ R E S O R T ■ S T Y
M I A M I ■ T R A Y S
■ A M U S E M E N T P A R K
■ G L A R E ■ E P E E S
J O B ■ A V E R T S ■ B E T
E T A ■ N E D ■ H U B C A P S
W O R L D ■ P E R I L
I O T A ■ J U L Y F O U R T H
S L E D ■ A M O R E ■ B O R E
H E R S ■ W A D E D ■ S W I M
```

CPSIA information can be obtained
at www.ICGtesting.com
Printed in the USA
LVOW11s2143071216
516247LV00001B/4/P